THE NORTH INDIAN PEASANT GOES TO MARKET

LEON SWARTZBERG, JR.

MOTILAL BANARSIDASS
Delhi :: Varanasi :: Patna

Indological Publishers and Booksellers
Head Office : 41-U.A., Bungalow Road, Delhi-110 007
Branches : 1. Chowk, Varanasi-1. (U.P.)
2. Ashok Rajpath, Patna-4 (BIHAR)

First Edition · Delhi, 1979

By Shantilal Jain, at Shri Jainendra Press,
A-45, Phase-I, Industrial Area, Naraina, New Delhi-110 028
Published by Narendra Prakash Jain, for Motilal Banarsidass,
Bungalow Road, Jawahar Nagar, Delhi-110 007

Whatsoever a man soweth, that shall he also reap.

Galatians VI:7

CONTENTS

PREFACE

As a graduate student in the anthropology department of Columbia University I was invited in late 1962 to join a project at Columbia — under the direction of Dr. Conrad M. Arensberg and Dr. Morton Klass — to conduct research in India on the adaptation of long-established agricultural communities to changes in the national economy, and the effects of these changes on traditional cultures. This project was being sponsored by the National Institute of Mental Health.

Dr. Arensberg and Dr. Morton Klass, the second in command of the project, both suggested that Bihar would furnish a productive area for research, because little or no work had been done there by American anthropologists. Field work there, it was thought, would improve the sample of Indian studies. Furthermore, since the inhabitants of the village in Trinidad which Dr. Klass had studied (1961) had emigrated from Bihar, it was felt that a study undertaken near their place of origin would be useful. This last consideration also played a part in narrowing the area of study to the vicinity of Patna, the capital of Bihar. A further consideration was that a research site near Patna would bring me into contact with Dr. Namadeshwar Prasad, Chairman of the Sociology Department of Patna University, with whom Dr. Arensberg was acquainted.

Access to a large city with adequate medical facilities and quick transportation out of the area, if need be, was an important personal concern because I was bringing with me my wife and our four children, from three to ten years of age.

The selection of a village had to meet certain criteria in order to facilitate participant-observation, the prime method employed for gathering data : (1) it must be geographically distinct; (2) it must number fewer than a thousand inhabitants. Geographical distinctness would provide a ready-made focus while a small population site would allow one investigator to encompass the work. As it turned out, the village selected had approximately five hundred residents. A third criterion was that the village contain a number of people who derived income from wage labor outside of the village.

A personal, but nevertheless important consideration, was that the village selected would afford adequate living quarters — something difficult to find in India, where houses do not remain unoccupied — for my family. Fortunately, in our second day of searching we were introduced through a friend of a friend to a local Block Development Officer who had some acquaintance with anthropology and well understood our problem. He announced flatly that he knew of a village which would meet our criteria. And so we discovered Phulia Tola, where we were to make our home for the next eighteen months, from January, 1964, to June, 1965.

The participant-observation method of doing field work was the most direct and, I believe, for this study the most effective. I lived as much as possible with the villagers and imitated their habits. I went with them on their daily rounds, whether to the fields or to the nearby town. No wedding in the village was complete without the Pandit, myself and my assistant. I did not, however, carry the participant part of participant-observation to ridiculous lengths : I did not plow a field, nor did I milk a cow; but I did eat with my right hand as Indians do, even in my own home. When I ate with the villagers I ate on the ground with them. I smoked the small Indian cigarettes, *bīrī*, and went to the men's songfests. At first I did these things to gain acceptance and, in the case of the songfests, because it was part of my job; but I soon became entranced by the songfests and addicted to the Indian cigarettes.

The village Headman's house in which I had our living quarters was located in one of the two major social centers of the village and was, therefore, well situated for observation. Many evenings, when I thought the day's activities had ended, silent white-clad figures would emerge from the gloom to settle on the Headman's verandah just a few feet away from my portals, and I would know a panchayat meeting was about to take place.

Participant-observation has, as I see it, two advantages : first, it allows the researcher to draw the natural connections between events in the culture. The steady stream of milk going to the nearby market town of Khagaul and the returning stream of goods are graphic evidence of the interaction of village and town. Second, participant-observation forces the researcher to pay attention to what the culture deems is important. The flurry of activity which accompanied the visit of an official to survey land deeds signaled the importance of possessing land. The visit of this official also revealed the existence of land documents which upon investigation proved to be of great importance in my efforts to trace the development of Phulia Tola. The concern of the villagers to have their land properly recorded and the disputes which arose at other times over the actual boundaries of plots are other visible examples of the interrelatedness of events.

Another important method of the field-work was interviewing. This was used to supplement observation and to gain information not available by observation. *Interview* is too formal a word to describe the actual situation; *conversation* would be more appropriate. Conversations took place in fields, in town, in my office, or walking down the road or jogging along on a horse-drawn cart — in short, anywhere at all. The conversations away from my house or office were, for the most part, taken down in long hand; those which took place in the house or the office were usually recorded on tape. There were, however, many occasions when the tape recorder was used to good advantage *in situ*. These interviews tended to be open-ended, wide-ranging affairs in which my net was spread widest to catch the inter-connections of events.

Land deeds, scanty village records, and some records from the town hall also yielded information pertaining to the life and history of the village.

The research design was simple and direct. My aim was to gather as much data about the village as possible, both synchronically and diachronically, with an emphasis on the latter. The reason for this emphasis was that the orientation of the project was towards social and cultural change resulting from interaction with influences outside the village. This orientation explains why the third criterion in choosing a village had to be met. The assumption was that contacts made outside the village would prove to be a significant factor in the life and development of the village.

For the purposes of this study it was not deemed necessary to arrive at an independent system of transliteration. English is still being used in the Patna area. It is usual to see Hindi names of streets and stores written in English. At the time I was in

Patna two Indian dailies were being published in English. Periodicals in English were also easily available. Thus a conventional spelling of Hindi proper names and common terms in English has arisen. Furthermore, anthropological literature has standardized many spellings, such as *panchayat* (assembly) and *gaon* (village). In these cases I have followed convention. In quoting documents I have left the spelling of Hindi names as they appear in the original, for while there is variation, the meaning is clear in every case. Hindi terms which are not common in the literature, I have spelled according to the system outlined in Basham (1954:xxl, 506 ff.).

Throughout this study monetary values are generally expressed in terms of rupees, the monetary unit of India. During my stay in Bihar two systems of exchange were operating. Under the older system sixteen annas equalled one rupee; under the present system the value of a rupee is one hundred pice, the anna having been officially discontinued although still in use. The official rate of exchange was 4.73 rupees to the dollar at the time the field-work was in progress. It is better, however, to think, as we did, of the rupee as equivalent to the dollar in terms of buying power.

We lived in the village for a period of eighteen months, from the beginning of 1964 to the middle of 1965.

The American myth of the "self-made man" readily dissolves when I think back to the many people who were instrumental in accomplishing the purpose of this dissertation. First among these is Dr. Conrad M. Arensberg who has been my mentor. My debt to him is large indeed. While I am indebted to Dr. Morton Klass for many things, I am particularly appreciative of his efforts in my behalf during my first weeks in India. It was he who suggested that I park my family with his wife, Sheila, and their two children in Asansol while we went to Patna to look for a village. Then, and many times since, he has made my problems his own.

B. N. Varma was helpful in preparing us for the problems we would face in India and in volunteering the services of his brother, N. Varma, who went to much trouble in helping us find the desired village. Dr. N. Prasad and the Sociology Department of Patna University provided us with an academic home. Dr. Walter Hauser and his wife, Rosemary, formed the American

Colony in Patna and were most generous in their hospitality.

So many Indians gave of their time and advice that it would be difficult to give separate thanks to all of them. There are, however, a few whom I would especially like to mention. Mr. Thakur Prasad, the Block Development Officer of Phulwari Sharif, was a good friend, and a source of information and help. He was the one who actually introduced us to the village. Dr. Adhaya Sharan of the Geography Department of Patna University became a good friend and an intellectual stimulant.

The Roy family supplied us with the essential ingredient for our stay : they converted their cowbarn into a *pukka* house for us, and they allowed us to become part of their joint family. The Secretary of the Gram Panchayat, Sheo Nandan Singh, gave me many valuable insights into village life and was unsparing of his time and friendship. Special thanks go to my interpreter-assistant, Rajat Kumar Agrawal, who brought great ability and devotion to our task. Suresh Roy was most helpful as a substitute assistant and in corresponding with me. It is to the people of the village that I give my final thanks.

I dedicate this dissertation to my wife, Patricia, and to our four children Sandy, Terry, Joanne, and Carolyn, who made a home away from home.

* * *

This work first appeared in 1969 as my doctoral dissertation. Now, ten years later, it is being published in order to make its findings more available to more people. For me the significant discovery in the research is that the development of a market place can aid and abet the creation of a peasant economy. If, as commonly thought, a peasant economy hinders a market economy, then the relationship of the two types of economy would present a problem for developing nations.

Ashland, Leon Swartzberg Jr.
Oregon 1979

SCHEMATIC MAP OF THE AREA

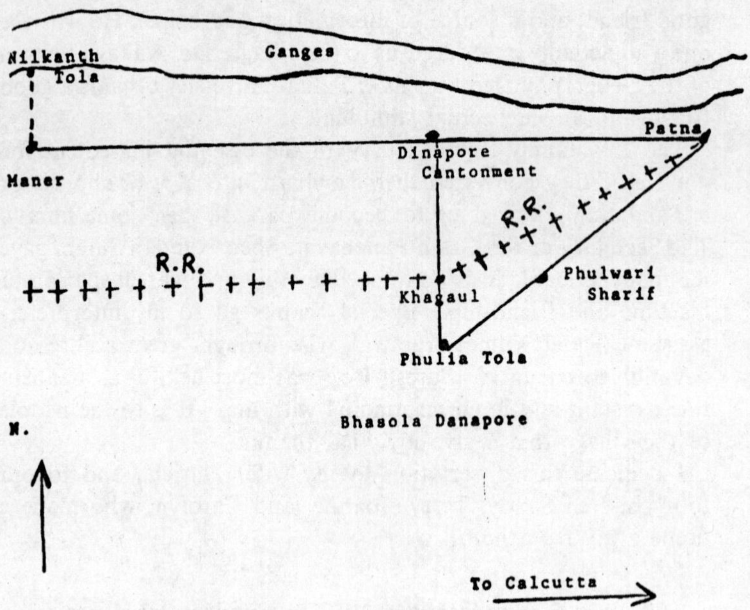

Distances :

Dinapore to Patna	8 miles
Dinapore to Maner	10 miles
Dinapore to Khagaul	3 miles
Khagaul to Phulia Tola	1 mile
Khagaul to Calcutta	340 miles
Phulia Tola to Phulwari Sharif	3 miles
Phulia Tola to Bhasola Danapore	1 mile

CHAPTER I

INTRODUCTION

India at the present time preserves a culture which in many respects has changed little during the past millennium. The center of this culture is the village. The village is representative of India, and the history of India is in a true sense the history of its villages. There the anthropologist expects to find the economic, political, and social patterns which give India its national character and which set it within the frame of history. It is particularly important to investigate both the forces which serve to maintain these patterns, as well as those which operate to change them.

Phulia Tola, where the writer spent eighteen months in 1963-1965, is one of the many villages which can be seen from the window of a train as it travels eastward towards Patna. It is situated on the flat alluvial plain of the Ganges approximately seven miles south of that river. About twenty miles to the west of the village is the Son River. At one time the Son or one of its tributaries flowed through what is now the western part of the village, and the old banks were still visible at the time of the writer's visit. The Patna canal forms the eastern border of the settlement site. In addition to benefiting from the high water table caused by the confluence of the rivers, the soil is favored by a rainfall which averages fifty inches annually, 85 per cent of it falling during the monsoon season from June to October. The temperature ranges from fifty-two degrees Fahrenheit in the evening during the cold season to one hundred and fifteen degrees during the heat of summer. The seasons are the hot season, from March to May; the rainy season, from June to October; and the cold season, from November to February. The soil of the area is noted for its fertility. Various grains and vegetables are cultivated, but the principal crop is rice.

The village is in many respects a typical North Indian village. Its inhabitants are all agriculturalists. As Hindus, they worship many of the all-India gods. They are governed by a *Panchayat* system, have a nucleated settlement pattern, practice caste endogamy and village exogamy, and follow North Indian customs of dress. The village is atypical in that all its inhabitants, with the exception of two families, belong to the same caste and sub-caste; in that all the castes which serve the village, with two exceptions, come from outside the village; and in that many of the villagers work as wage laborers in the neighboring towns. Also atypical is the existence of a family in the village, the Roys, which is not only far wealthier than the other families of the village but which also, significantly, derives its income from a business enterprise outside the village.

A mile from Phulia Tola is the nearest town, Khagaul, which provides a market economy that has close ties with the economy of the village. The intent of this work is to examine the relationship of Khagaul and its market economy with Phulia Tola and its peasant economy. The emphasis will be on the village and the changes which have taken place in its approximately one hundred years of existence through its contact with the town. Particular attention will be given to the village economy. Economic patterns of behavior, such as householding and marketing, though conceptually distinct, interrelate at many points, as will be seen from the very history of the village.

Since the village is of fairly recent origin, much of its history is known, and the process of its formation and growth is essentially clear.

The historical development of the village and various aspects of economic and other cultural relationships in Phulia Tola are described to a large extent in terms of the history, the interests, and the attitudes of the most important family in the village, the Roys. The separateness of the Roys from the village and, at the same time, their domination of the village would have required, in any case, careful investigation of them. The very fact of the Roys' exclusive ability to provide living quarters for us — and their willingness to do so — was indicative of the Roys' unique position in the village and the important part they had inevitably to play in an analysis of the village. The interest of the writer in the Roys, however, first came about as the result of happenstance.

Since the writer and his family had occupied quarters provided by the Roys and since the quarters adjoined those of the Roys, it was to be expected that our hosts would be our first acquaintances in the village. And when, shortly after his arrival in the village, it was ascertained that the writer had a slipped disc, the resultant immobility dictated that the natural process of getting acquainted with our hosts should go hand in hand with the scientific investigation of them. As their story of rags to riches in the space of two generations unfolded, it became apparent that they were by far the richest family in Phulia Tola and perhaps for miles around, and that they presented a contrast to the other villagers. Certain questions, therefore, inevitably came to mind : What was the secret of their success ? In what ways were the Roys like other families in the village; in what way different from them ?

The answers to these questions raised certain conceptual and theoretical problems : What type or types of economies were operating in the village ? If there was more than one, what was their relationship to each other ? What part had the market played in shaping the economy or economies ? Was there a developmental pattern ? These questions led to consideration of a basic problem. If, as the writer suspected, there was another economy operating in conjunction with the obvious market economy, was it a peasant economy ? Then, finally, what was a peasant ?

The thesis argued here is that the village of Phulia Tola contains two economies — market and household; that for most of the village the household economy prevails; that the presence of the household economy inhibits the operation of the market economy although the latter partially supports the household economy and, in some instances, is an aid in the formation of a household economy. Finally, the dissertation will consider the relevance of the concept of householding to any definition of the peasant.

Underlying these theses are the assumptions of Malinowski and Polanyi concerning the unity of all aspects of culture and the embeddedness of the economy in the culture. Basic to all anthropological studies is the concept of the unity of the various institutions of culture. While these can be isolated for purposes of classification and comparison, misunderstanding and incorrect analysis inevitably result when cultural institutions are studied as disparate phenomena. The interrelationship of all aspects of culture was a major theme in the works of Bronislaw Malinowski and constitutes an important contribution to anthropological theory :

> All departments of tribal life, religion, magic, economics are interwoven, but the *social organization* of the tribe lies at the foundation of everything else [1922:69].

Malinowski was particularly conscious of this relationship in man's economic activities. Speaking of the Trobriand Islander, he says :

> He works prompted by motives of a highly complex, social and traditional nature, and towards aims which are certainly not directed towards the satisfaction of present wants, or to the direct achievement of utilitarian purposes [ibid:60].

The concepts of Bronislaw Malinowski and Richard Thurnwald before him regarding the relationship of economics to anthropological studies have been seminal. The new point of view about economic anthropology was asserted first in *Trade and Markets in the Early Empires*, edited by Karl Polanyi, Conrad M. Arensberg and Harry W. Pearson :

> The human economy ... is embedded and enmeshed in institutions, economic and non-economic. The inclusion of the non-economic is vital [Polanyi, 1957b:250].

Like Malinowski, Arensberg also emphasizes the underlying social structure :

> Anthropology is deeply committed to this priority of social patterns in any scheme for the understanding of the substantive economies of the human record. ... Anthropology expects the social arrangement underlying economic behaviors and motives to be particular human inventions of historical times and places [1957:100-101].

This study follows the new orientation and gives support to it. Accordingly, the village economy is conceived throughout as functioning within thc socio-cultural matrix of village life. Consequently, the behavioral patterns which characterize and are integral to the peasant economy of an Indian village are all shown to be correlated with the non-economic patterns of village culture.

This dissertation rests on one other assumption: history is necessary to support and explain processual analysis.[1] In his comprehensive article "Anthropology as History," Arensberg has explained why the reliance on history is methodologically sound and necessary:

> Each term of the analysis leading to these findings must have particular, empirical, historical documentation. Moreover, once this proof can be provided we can at once go on further to depicting the processes which have given us the actual events of the past emergence of these institutions. It is in this way alone, in treating them as culture traits, that we can legitimately spell out the cultural dynamics and reconstruct the true history of economic institutions. This dynamics and this rewon history is the best account we will ever have of their "origins" [1957:107].

The history of the village must be looked upon as part of the history of greater India; village events can be understood only within the context of that nation's development. The writer has, therefore, cited the facts of Indian economic and social history wherever they are pertinent to the topic under consideration to show the inter-relationship of the little community of Phulia Tola and the larger community of India.

In completing the following study it was found necessary to clarify certain terms and phenomena which heretofore have been inadequately defined or described. The word "peasant" in particular has been difficult to define because the anthropological literature is still in the discovery phase with regard to peasantry (Foster, 1967:2-14). The following schema will serve as a guide to the analysis of the subject.

---

1. I can use with confidence oral history and written history to complement each other, for where the accounts overlap they confirm each other in all cases. For example, I was told that Phulia Devi, the founder of the village, had to move her house to make way for the canal. When one account gave a date for the canal which would make it precede or contemporaneous with her arrival, I was disappointed with the discrepancy but dismissed it as not being important. However, another document established that I had confused one canal for another and that the one which skirts the village was completed well after Phulia Devi's coming to the area.

I. Internal (Householding)
    A. Structure
        1. Domestic family unit

    B. Function
        1. Social-psychological
        2. Economic
            a) Production
            b) Distribution
            c) Consumption
        3. Political
            a) Control of domestic family unit

II. External (Part-Whole Relationship)
    A. Structure
        1. Domestic family unit
        2. Larger entity (than domestic family unit)

    B. Function
        1. Political
            a) Dominion
                (1) Force
                (2) Legality
                    (a) Title
        2. Economic
            a) Tribute
                (1) In kind
                (2) In cash
                    (a) market exchange

Certain family relationships and movements relevant to this study lack descriptive terms in anthropological literature. For these the writer has devised the following terms : (1) *gyno-consanguineal,* to describe the relationship of ego to any female blood relative; (2) *gyno-consanguine-local,* to describe movement by way of gyno-consanguineals; (3) *gyno-local,* to describe movement by way of female relatives.

CHAPTER II

THE ORIGINS OF THE VILLAGE

Geographical

The events and circumstances to be described center on the following places: the villages of Nilkanth Tola, Phulwari Sharif, and Phulia Tola; the towns of Dinapore and Khagaul; and the city of Patna.[1] Patna is the capital of the State of Bihar and of the above-named places is the most easterly. Patna and Dinapore lie eight miles apart along a main road which skirts the Ganges.

Dinapore (also known as Danapore) is famous as the cantonment whose troops were actively engaged in the Sepoy Mutiny of 1857. The inhabitants of the area usually refer to Dinapore as "The Cantonment." The main road connects the Cantonment with Khagaul three miles to the south. Since the advent of the Eastern Railway in 1863 (Davidson, 1868:181), there has been some confusion between Dinapore and Khagaul, for the rail-road station at Khagaul is officially named Dinapore. Following local usage, this paper will refer to Dinapore station as Khagaul. Like Patna, it is on the main line of the Eastern Railway to Calcutta, and is 340 miles, or an overnight journey, from that city.

An ancient dirt road connects Khagaul with the village of Phulia Tola and continues southward. From the pounding of the steadily increasing traffic of pedestrians, bicycles, horse-drawn wagons, ox-carts and animals over the past ten years, the road has sunk in places a few feet below the surrounding terrain. In the dry season it forms a blanket of dust, and a muddy morass when the monsoon comes.

Khagaul and Phulia Tola are vertices at the narrow base of an obtuse triangle whose apex is Patna. Three miles from Phulia Tola in the direction of Patna, the ancient town of Phulwari Sharif is located. A badly paved road connects Phulia Tola,

1. The spelling of proper nouns is as found in English language publications and documents. It is not a transliteration. Hindi terms are spelled phonetically as given in Basham (1954 : xxl, 50 ff.) or as is traditional in the literature.

Phulwari and Patna. Maner lies ten miles west of the Cantonment; about two to three miles north of Maner along the bank of the Ganges lies the site where the village of Nilkanth Tola once stood. The dirt road which formerly led there has narrowed to a path.

Nilkanth Tola, like many villages which dot the banks on either side of the Ganges, stood on *diara* land. Diara is the name applied to land which is either on the bank of the Ganges or which forms an island or a peninsula in the river itself. Because of the ebb and flow of the river, capriciously removing soil here and depositing it there, the fertility of diara land is extremely variable. O'Malley reports in 1907 that rents in the diara vary from R. 30 to 12 annas per acre (ibid. : 126), which means that the most expensive land costs forty times the cheapest. The people concerned with here would be those who rented land at the lower figure — land fit only for growing corn and grazing cattle and as such the refuge of poor families.[1] You can infer a person's social position from the food he eats : rice indicates he is well-to-do, maize that he is poor (O'Malley, 1907:48, 94). According to a survey of Buchanan, quoted by Mukerjee, "the poorest people in North Bihar and Bengal could not afford the daily use of rice [Mukerjee, 194 ? : 55]."

The writer once asked one of his friends in the area why a certain woman had moved into the village from the *diara* area, only to have the man rebuke him for asking about an event which had occurred before he was born and of which he could, therefore, have no knowledge. However, he suggested with a faint smile, she might have gotten tired of eating corn. Food continues to be a means of social distinction. During his entire stay in India the writer was never — either in village or town — served corn, though it is grown locally. He once bought some from a roadside stand but found it almost inedible.

In the diara area, people got along without good agricultural land; cows supplied milk and *ghee* (clarified butter) which they either consumed or bartered, and sold for grain and other necessities. Bulls and oxen were sold at the various animal fairs.

1. Since the *diara* has places where the soil is extremely fertile, and since the people of the village only referred to the *diara* as a place of poor soil, it may be concluded that the people of the village had only occupied the latter type of land.

Nor was ownership or tenancy essential on the least desirable land of the diara since it was abundant and fit only for grazing. Given the sparse population of the early 1800's (Davis, 1951:25) and the low level of technology, cattle raising made possible an efficient adaptation to this type of environment :

> The grazing animals, with digestive systems that are enormous in proportion to their size, do have the capacity to subsist on feeds too bulky and poor to nourish a human. Where the environment ... affords vegetable stuffs not directly nourishing to man but capable of sustaining some grazing animal, the adoption of a pastoral economy constitutes an advance in man's capacity to exploit the area. ... In all such areas individual animals or herds compete with one another ... but not with any other type of economy or land use ... With grazing animals ... even under primitive conditions ... there is a great range, 10:1 or even 100:1, between the largest herd a given labor force can care for and the smallest herd that would support that labor force.

Furthermore :

> Because of their mobility, herd animals can evade climate vicissitudes that would result in complete failure of a vegetable crop [Aschmann, 1965:265ff.].

William Buyers, writing in 1848, gives us a picture of this section of the country :

> From Mongher to Patna, the country is everywhere well cultivated, and populous, and very rich in cattle, with large herds of which the alluvial banks and islands thrown up by the river, are covered. But where a good soil has been deposited by the floods during the rains, it is ploughed and owned, as soon as the inundation has subsided, and produces beautiful crops ... Even the cattle, which graze on the banks and islands of the Ganges, as well as their owners, seem to be nearly amphibious. The large herd of milk cows and buffaloes that graze during the day on the little islands generally return to the villages on the mainland, every evening, to be milked and to spend the night.

> The herd-boy, or man, drives them all into the river before him, and then, with one hand, seizes the tail of a cow, or buffalo, and flourishing his stick in the other, is dragged along till they have reached the other side. He continues all the way shouting to them, in order to direct their course to the proper landing place, which they are occasionally in danger of missing, and being, consequently, carried too far down the current. Sometimes the herdsman mounts on the back of one of his charges, but the more usual way is to allow himself to be dragged along by the tail of one of the hindermost [pp. 169-170].

At that time nobody cared where cattle grazed; waste land abounded; but someday it would matter and cause trouble.

As already indicated, much of the diara was the refuge of poor people, for with a little land, usually on a share-cropper basis and with free pasturage for the cattle, a poor family could eke out a living. The risks were the vagaries of the river (though it eliminated the threat of drought) and the prevalence of cattle disease; the only direct expense was the initial cost of the cattle. But here Indian tradition came to the rescue of a poor man.

Cattle can be raised on *batai* basis. *Batai* literally means "division". It works in the following manner. Munga Lall gives an animal to Sita Ram to raise for him. After the cow gives birth, Sita brings the cow and the calf back to Munga Lall. The two men then valuate the cow and calf together, for a cow is of value only when a calf has freshened it. They then come to an agreement concerning ownership of the two animals. If Munga Lall, the owner, wants them, he pays half their value to Sita Ram for his expense in raising the animals. If Sita Ram, the man who raised them, wants the animals, he purchases them from Munga Lall for half their value. This system automatically insures a fair valuation of the animals; it also provides a way for a poor man to get a cow or water buffalo cheaply.

The story of Phulia Tola begins in the mid 1800's in the lowlands of the diara area around Maner, approximately twenty miles north and west from the highlands of the present-day village of Phulia Tola, from whence almost all the inhabitants of Phulia Tola or their forebears had emigrated. At the present time there are at least fourteen villages around Maner whose populations are made up exclusively or predominantly of the same Gowāllā caste that inhabits Phulia Tola. In his district gazetteer of 1907, O'Malley locates a particular segment of this selfsame caste in the north-western part of Maner. Life on the diara is precarious, for the Ganges as it changes its course from time to time both "giveth and taketh away"; what you are plowing today may be under water tomorrow. This was explained to the writer by a former villager of Nilkanth Tola as they stood on the bank in the growing dusk, and he sadly pointed to the spot in the river where Nilkanth Tola had once been. Generations ago, ironically, the forebears of the inhabitants of Nilkanth Tola had, themselves, moved to the southern bank of the river when the river changed its course and flooded them out (Lacy, 1931:33).

Social

With the exception of three families, the inhabitants of Phulia Tola belong to the same caste, Yādava, commonly pronounced Yādo, and sub-caste, Krishnaut, a name which to them denotes descent from Lord Krishna. The sub-caste is the endogamous group. As far back as is known, the Yādava were called Gowāllā (or one of its variants, Goāllā, Goyāllā, Gopā, Goālā), a name derived from Hindi *gai*, or *go*, which means "cow" and *wāllā* which is roughly translated as "he who does". Hence, *Gowāllā* means "he who has to do with cows," or "cowherder," or "milk-man," as the natives tell you today. *Ahir* is another one of the caste names.

It is, therefore, reasonable to conclude that cowherding has been and continues to be the traditional occupation of the Gowāllās (or Yādavas). Nevertheless, with them, as with many other castes in India, agriculture has become an additional if not the main means of gaining a livelihood. The Census of India for 1911 notes that "many village artisans are also partly dependent on agriculture" and that "there is a tendency for those persons to abandon their hereditary occupation in favor of farming (Anon., 1911 : 415)." This point is emphasized by Martin (whose writings were based on the observations of the famous surveyor Francis Hamilton Buchanan) with reference to the Gowāllās in Patna District as early as 1811 :

> Although the proper duties of the tribe are to tend cattle, of the buffalo and cow kind, and prepare and sell milk, by

> far the greater part in this district are mere farmers, and hold the plough [1838:168].
>
> . . . .
>
> Goyālās that prepare and sell milk ... form a very small part of this numerous tribe [ibid.:300].

Edward T. Dalton in 1872 furnished significant facts about the manner of life of this caste during the nineteenth century :

> Immense numbers of Ahirs or Gopas still cling to the nomadic life of their ancestors. Seeking the high grazing grounds of Central India and Western Bengal they form encampments of the pasture lands where they reside with their wives, families, and herds till the grass in the neighborhood is exhausted, subsisting entirely on the proceeds of their milk and butter. The houses they use are constructed on large bamboo mats; they can be taken to pieces and removed like tents.
>
> But a still larger section of the tribe have quite given up this wandering life, and forming permanent villages have settled down as good farmers and cultivators, only distinguishable from other agriculturists by a possession of larger herds of cattle, by the greater care bestowed on them and in profiting more by the sale of butter and milk [1960:302ff.].
>
> . . . .
>
> They are found as extensive farmers. ... They do not however forsake their hereditary calling; they keep large herds of buffaloes and cows, and freely sell the milk and butter; the latter in the form of *ghee*. They live very generally in village communities and have their hereditary village headman, who with a council of village elders decides all questions of caste [ibid.:303 ff.].

Dalton notes above that Gowāllās live in single-caste communities. Habib feels that during the Mughal's time single-caste communities were the rule and adds, "This is true of many villages today (1963:122)". Phulia Tola is an example of such a one-caste village. (Anthropologists, it seems, have tended to concentrate their studies on multi-caste villages).

It is important to note that Martin's description pertaining specifically to Patna District, the area under review, is of an early date. Dalton's quotation, however, even though it does not refer to the Ganges plain, makes the point that agriculture was incorporated into (rather than substituted for, as Martin implies) the already existing herding and milking occupations. This agrees with both the writer's observations and the data furnished by the censuses of India concerning principal and subsidiary means of livelihood. When farming was added to herding, the new was added to the old. This development follows Romer's rule in paleontology, "to conserve the old in the face of change [Arensberg, 1966:211]." The process of conservation and combination is the mechanism by which the people of Phulia Tola adapted themselves to various cultural-ecological niches. Dalton has described the initial adaptation, the settling down of the nomadic Gowāllās to cultivation along with herding. The second stage, the large-scale participation in and adaptation of the market to an agricultural economy, will form the principal subject of this paper. To construct a simple paradigm : in the first stage, agriculture is new and herding is old; in the second stage, agriculture is old and the market is new. Each stage illustrates conservation and adaptation.

As a group, the Gowāllās, despite some improvement in their condition, continue to be a poor caste. The Indian Government lists them as a Backward Caste. Dalton tells us in 1872 :

> All the authorities are agreed in assigning to the Gopas a high place among Sudras, though there may be a difference as to whether all the tribes of the pastoral family are entitled to so honourable a position [1960:302].

Dutt in 1884 described those in Bengal as Sudras (Dutt, 1884: 90), while the Census of India in 1901 classified them as clean Sudras (Gatt, 1902:374). Martin, however, referred to those in the area around Patna as "the lowest of the Sudras" but added that "at their hands a pure Brahman can drink without disgrace [loc. cit.]." Srinivas (1962:24, 58), Bailey (1957:188), Beidelman (1959:15), and Davis (1951:107 ff.) maintain that ritual status and the economic condition of a caste are correlated. It was, therefore, no mere coincidence that the impoverished Gowāllās of the nineteenth century belonged to the class of Sudras. Or to put it within the context of this paper, the economic is embedded within the social and religious. The Gowāllās have claimed higher ritual status, Kshatriya, as they earned a better livelihood; they then called themselves Yādava, and the first to adopt the symbols were prosperous families such as the Roys.

In common with most parts of North India, it is customary for girls to marry men who live in other villages and to reside virilocally. People of your village have a fictive relationship with you; people of the same generation are your village brothers and sisters; people older than yourself are your village aunts and uncles, and so forth. When a girl marries, her share of her family's property is represented by the *tilak* (dowry) which is transferred to her husband's family at the time of her marriage. By village custom she ordinarily inherits nothing more because the family feels that their obligation to her has then ceased. However, if her father has no sons, he may ask, or, as the Indians say, "call" a daughter and her husband to come and live with him, with the tacit understanding that the son-in-law will inherit upon his father-in-law's death. Similarly, a family will reclaim its daughter, especially if she has no male children to inherit her husband's share of the property. A similar "call" or invitation may be extended to a married woman by a brother who has no male heir and is alone; or, as we shall see in the case of the Roy family, a woman may adopt her brother's child if she has no children of her own.

When an Indian male activates a female connection, as in moving to his wife's family, or to his mother's family, or to his sister's family, it is to improve his position, for in northern India inheritance is through the male line. Ordinarily, he "stays put" and does not move from his village unless there is nothing to inherit or the possibilities of inheriting through female connections outside the village, are living where he resides. Female links can be even more distant than those just mentioned. One of the early settlers came to Phulia Tola through his wife's sister who had married into the village. In a more recent case, a woman who had been born and raised in her father's village was accepted with her sick husband into her mother's natal household. Upon the death of her husband, she in turn called in her daughter and son-in-law to set up a joint household with her.

In northern India, village exogamy, caste endogamy, and caste in-group feeling create a horizontal solidarity of caste which cuts across village ties of unity (Srinivas, 1962:75, 98; 1963:9, 11, 12) and links together members of the same caste residing in different localities. Mayer has shown how caste links — sub-castes in his terms — have territoriality with uterine and affinal links (1960:6). In other words, it is the wife or daughter who maintains sub-caste solidarity and sub-caste connections; for in a patrilineal, patrilocal society, as we have here, contacts with relatives living outside the village are maintained only through them. Thus when a family thinks about moving out of its own village, it will first survey the affinals. The women of a family thus provide a path for migration.

Ordinarily an Indian will only move to a place where he is known; he will have a relative there, a relative who will invite him, provide house-room or land and generally ease his way and be responsible for him. This was explained to the writer by an old inhabitant of Phulia Tola :

> If anyone comes from any place, he lives with his relatives. If Kitab Lall had come here with only his buffalo and his cow, and if he needs fifty rupees on the day he arrives in the new village, then who will have the money ? If any relation of mine asks any help from me, as Kitab Lall has asked, I will give as much as I can. ... How can he buy without knowing anything about the land ? He can buy land and a house in the city without knowing anyone, but he can't buy in the village. I don't know anything about that place; how can I buy the land ? How can I go from here to that place for plowing ? It will have to be on a rental basis. ... Our civilization is such that if I want to purchase something, I must ask and get suggestions from my relatives living there. Or my friends. He won't buy all of a sudden.*

Another man said :

> Generally when people flee from any place, they have to go to their relatives. Land is arranged for farming and houses are built. You just can't move suddenly. First

*Translated from Hindi.

> you move to a relative; then you look for another village and settle there.*

The writer asked a recent arrival if he would have come to the village without an invitation and received the following reply :

> Where my relations are, I go there. The people who do not have any trouble — they offer money to me and say, come live with us.*

Visiting in and going to other villages where there are kin is an important Indian practice; in this way ties between families and villages are maintained. Noticeable activity of this sort occurs during the wedding season when groups of men go to other villages in search of mates for their sons and daughters. They will go to villages where they have relations or relations of relations. Or they may be acquainted with relatives of their close friends. Marriage celebrations are, of course, occasions for people to gather from outside villages. The same is true of funeral ceremonies. Women do a lot of visiting, for they are always going back and forth to see their own families or to visit married sisters. Fathers and brothers call on their married female relatives. Men of related families see each other for many reasons : to purchase a cow, to borrow money, or to get a job. Someone is always coming to or going from a village. It is easier to identify the female than the male visitor, for she travels in *purdah* : the vehicle — pony cart, ox cart, rickshaw, or the occasional car — is invariably curtained to shield her from view.

When a woman travels she is accompanied by a man, usually her brother, for ideally there is a special bond between brother and sister. In northern India this bond is formalized in a special ceremony and celebration.

Apart from ceremonial occasions, visiting among consanguineals and friends is less formal than in the United States. No preparation is needed for the visitor; a little more food is cooked, an extra cot is brought out or some child doubles up, or a mattress is put on the floor. During his stay the "guest" will become a regular member of the family and share in its usual tasks. Once when Ram Chendra, who as the oldest male of my host's family

---

*Translated from Hindi.

normally supervised the cultivation, fell ill, a relative who happened to be visiting took over his job. No one told him to do this; and he stayed at the job for months.

Women have a tendency to spend more time away from home than men. This is especially true of new brides, who spend long periods at their natal home as part of their transition to married life. Women as a rule are freer than men to absent themselves from the village because men are needed to do the heavy work in the fields. There are exceptions, however, especially when men's services are required to fulfill family obligations outside the village. The writer knows of one man, for example, who stayed with his brother-in-law for a year in order to help him in a business venture. During that year he was treated as a regular member of the family, getting his food, clothing, and the like, but no wages as such. Often children are sent to relatives because better facilities for schooling are available in their area. Such children help around the house and farm, just like the family children.

A marriage system which promotes extensive village ties (Srinivas, 1963:12), with its concomitant visiting pattern, is conducive to migration, for it provides choice of location, and hence condition, and risks few leaps into the unknown (Klass, 1966:959-961). Anthropological studies of India reveal a tendency to deal with society as static, but movement and process and change are characteristic of life in general and of the Indian village especially. Neale goes so far as to say :

> The type of village is ancient, but actual villages have had short histories in the constant process of founding, conquest, destruction, and depopulation [1962:47].

Habib's comments, although descriptive of Mughal times, are equally valid today :

> There were ... always stretches of virgin land beckoning to the peasant, while with his low level of subsistence and primitive huts he had no immovable possessions to tie him to his old place of habitation, ... This capacity of mobility

> on the part of the peasants must be regarded as one of the most striking features of the social and economic life of the times. It was the peasant's first answer to famine of man's oppression [1963:116 ff.].

A glance at the section on internal migration in any British census of India will confirm the relevance of Habib's observation for the period under discussion. More pertinent, however, are Dalton's remarks relative to the nomadic life of the Gowāllās. Karve, incidentally, ascribes the origin of caste mainly to migration (1961:15 ff., 116). Dr. Adhya Sharan of the Geography Department of Patna University shares the view that migration is a salient feature of Indian life. He compares American pioneers with Indian pioneers, but with this difference : the pioneer in America pushed westward into virgin territory; the Indian pioneer settled on vacant lands between villages. Dr. Sharan noted this as particularly true of the Gowāllās because of their poverty. While an ample literature exists on the subject of urbanization, little can be found on "ruralization," the movement from village to village or from town to village. Regarding such movements in the Patna District, O'Malley reports that "there is a tendency for the village population to increase while that of the towns declines [1907:45]." The village of Phulia Tola furnishes evidence for the penetration and development of such an Indian pioneer village.

The extensive marriage network in a country where arable land is scarce played an important part in the emergence of the village. Mayer finds an increasing tendency to activate female lines when arable land is in demand (1960:245). This applies to Phulia Tola : the vast majority of the families migrated to the village via female connection. And while other factors, such as the market, were involved in the movement, the primary one was the desire for land. The village would appear particularly attractive to a poor caste such as the Gowāllās living alongside the Ganges. It must be remembered that land in the village, as contrasted with the diara land was high land, safe from the vicissitudes of the river. It was, furthermore, as soon as the trees would be cut down, potentially good land. In a country where the amount and quality of land possessed is a criterion of prestige, the motivation for the migration to the village was the availability of land. As a recent commentary shows, the demand for land in Bihar was significant :

> It thus seems established that an increase in cultivation since Mughal times has taken place everywhere, though in varying degrees. The increase is the greatest, amounting to about a hundred per cent in three regions. The first region comprises Ilahabad, Awadh and Bihar, and, possibly, parts of Bengal [Habib, 1963:22].

Already in the nineteenth century, as Moreland and Chatterjee point out, there was strong evidence of "the emergence of competition for productive land" resulting in "a scramble for land (1945:382)." The consequences of this scramble were noted at the time by Hunter :

> As cultivation advances, the area of waste land available for grazing steadily diminishes, and the prospects of the poor beasts are becoming worse rather than better [Hunter, 1886:519 ff.].

The effect of the increase in tillage and the decrease in pasturage will be seen in microcosm in this study of an Indian village.

Economic

As explained above, a poor man could earn a living by grazing cows on the diara or other barren land and by trading and selling milk. Both Martin and Dalton established that this situation prevailed as far back as the first half of the eighteenth century. One way for a poor herdsman to acquire ownership of a cow was provided by the system known as "batai." There were, however, other means to this end. If a man lived close to a market, he might induce some rich man to give him "advance money." This means that the lender advances the purchase price of the cow or water buffalo and the debtor pays off the debt by supplying milk to the lender. The English have been in the area since 1765, and the men of Phulia Tola assured the writer that they and their fathers have sold milk to the British on the advance money basis since 1900. The writer assumes, then, that "advance money" is an old practice. The writer himself, was a party to this kind of deal when he lived in the village. The natives, incidentally, liked to get advance money from the British, for when an English creditor moved, he would forgive the unpaid part of the debt as *baksheesh* (a tip).

The cheapest way to acquire cattle was theft. Among the Gowāllās theft and robbery seem, in fact, to constitute a significant cultural pattern :

> The Goyalas ... in many parts are not only accused of unfair dealing in their trade; but are suspected of being addicted to theft and robbery [Martin, 1838:168].
>
> The Aheers, or Goalahs, form the herdsman class. They are turbulent and dishonest, and are regularly retained as *lattials*, or clubmen by the rich [Dutt, 1884:90].
>
> The Goalas, or Ahirs ... are notoriously the most quarrelsome caste in the district, constantly concerned in riots, and very fond of the lāthi [club]; cattle trespass forms a frequent subject of dispute among them. They have the reputation of being audacious cattle stealers, and many at the bottom of the social scale are professional thieves [O'Malley, 1907:50 ff.]. . . . .
>
> The Goālās are continually engaged in ... petty thefts of crops from granaries and fields, and they seldom lose an opportunity of grazing their cattle on a neighbor's crops. They are even more notorious for cattle-lifting, which they practice with equal boldness and success [ibid.:164].
>
> [Goālās] are usually cultivators and cattle-breeders, and have a bad reputation for fighting over disputes regarding cattle-trespass [James, 1914:12].

The analysis of cattle trespass, another significant pattern, will be undertaken later.

Milk, ghee, butter and the cattle from which these come play an important part in this account; for the story of Phulia Tola is the story of the Gowāllās, and as Gowāllās they always have been concerned with these items. This is clear from the quoted comments of Buyers, Martin, Dalton, Dutt, O'Malley, and James. Martin even remarks that the different "classes" (sub-castes) make butter in different ways (1838:341). As long as people can remember, milk has been collected from a circle of villages. Either the milk was brought to a center or people from the center went out and gathered the milk from the perimeter. The milk was brought to market in earthen or brass jars, or in leather bags, all suspended at the ends of long bamboo rods which were balanced on the shoulders of men who covered the distance from village to town at a rapid trot-like gait. The same system continues today except that, in place of jars or bags, kerosene tins are used.

Even before the completion of the railroads and the Suez canal in the nineteenth century, India had national and international markets (Habib, 1963:61-89; Leeds, 1961). This trade was carried on land by caravans, on rivers by barges and boats, and along the coast by ships (Radhakamal, 194 ?:118). What is of interest to us is that butter and ghee were regularly carried and that Patna and Dinapore were noted for their ports and as import-export centers for Agra and Calcutta (Radhakamal, 194 ?: passim; Habib, 1963:63, 73). Martin places the trade centers even closer to the area under consideration :

> On this part of the Ganges, Danapur and Digha are the only places in these districts which carry on an export and import trade by water [1838:7].

"The Ganges ... has always been the great line of traffic from earliest times [O'Malley, 1907:44]." But before the rail-roads, prices in India tended to be regional (Radhakamal, 194 ?:41). In this regard, it is important to note that during the Mughal period the price of ghee was lowest in Bihar and that the quality of its milk was praised (Habib, 1963:84, 84 ff.). Even if supply and demand worked imperfectly, the low price and the high quality signify the existence of a plentiful supply of milk during the Mughal period. Buyers' 1948 description of the Gowāllās as raising large herds gives further support to this conclusion.

Undoubtedly local markets were early integrated with regional markets; this integration had the effect of transferring demand for milk from the regional markets, which were connected with each other along the Ganges, to the small Gowāllā villages in and around the diara even before the advent of the rail-road in 1857-1863. To the regional demand for milk must be added the local demand of the nearby town of Patna, Dinapore, Khagaul, and Phulwari Sharif.

Martin describes Dinapore about fifty years after it was founded (Houlton, 1949:26) :

> Danapur is by far the principal place, and independent of the military, and the followers attached to the corps, and those that accompany them, contains a great many people. In different market places scattered within the boundaries of the cantonment, and under military authority are said to be 3,236 houses. These markets are rather better built than usual country towns, and afford many more comforts for the Europeans than Patna, which in that respect is a very wretched place; *the gentlemen who reside in Patna are supplied with almost every necessary from Danapur.* .... The military buildings are very grand especially ... and the grounds round them are well laid out, while the roads in the vicinity, and through the cantonments, are tolerable, so that the whole appearance is superior to Patna [1838:45. Italics supplied].

Milk and butter were some of the necessities supplied from Dinapore and environs.

Henry E. Fane, a traveler passing through in 1835, comments, "[The] appearance of the town [was] far superior to Patna [1842:41]." He refers to the 3,236 houses said to have been there in 1811, the year of Francis Hamilton Buchanan's visit. By multiplying the number of houses in Dinapore (3,236) by five, Edward Thornton arrives at an estimated population, exclusive of the military, of 16,130. Thornton also supplies the figures 284,132 for the population of Patna and 1,200,000 for Patna District (1857:282).

John Snow, writing in 1848, concurs with Martin and Faim in his discussion of Dinapore :

> Altogether the place has quite a military aspect, and more of a European character than any other of the stations, on this part of the Ganges [1848:205].

Martin also tells us something about Phulwari Sharif, just three miles from Phulia Tola :

> Phulwari ... is a good country, containing 1700 houses, one of brick and many of them, although constructed of mud, have two stories, are covered with tiles, and are very large. These belong chiefly to Muhammedans of rank and education [loc. cit.].

The figures for 1811 listed below afford some idea of the commerce in milk products.[1] Unfortunately the writer has no way of knowing the quantities represented, but the figures themselves are impressive, both specifically and comparatively.

Milk : R. 10,000 Patna City and all the other districts : No export, all import.

Ghi or Boiled Butter : Patna City and all districts : R. 207,750 — import. Export : R. 80,480.

Ghi or Boiled Butter : Patna City, Import : R. 184,250. Export : Rs. 71,600 [Martin 1838:41, Appendix].

In Martin's complete list only four items show a greater total for combined import and export. These items are opium, salt (two types), wheat, and rice. Obviously there was a large trade in dairy products.

With the coming of the East India Railway to the Patna Dinapore area in 1857 (Thornton, 1857:282), Calcutta was transformed from a remote to a local market. Over the line which joined the two cities, milk, butter and ghee were transported from the Patna area to Calcutta overnight. Since Indian dairy products have a lower butterfat content than ours and consequently keep longer, refrigeration was not necessary.

In 1857 the terminal was Patna City, six miles east of present-day Patna and the principal place at that time (ibid.). In 1863 the Son River was bridged, the station at Khagaul opened (known officially as Dinapore Station), and the rail-road extended to Benares. For all practical purposes all of North India was linked together by rail in 1868. In 1866 fifteen trains were moving each way almost daily, indicating that the volume of goods carried was high (Davidson, 1868:181). The railway made all of North India one market; and when the Suez canal opened in 1869, North India became part of the world market.

1. Martin's writings are based upon Buchanan's reports of 1811.

The effect of the railroad on the commerce of Khagaul was immediate and far reaching :

> The Dinapur railway station is just outside the town, which indeed has only sprung into importance since the opening of the railway [Hunter, 1885:122, Vol. 8].
>
> Much of the trade from the south which formerly came to Dinapore has been taken from it by Khagaul, a town which rose in importance at the coming of the railway. Khagaul has now a population of 6,000. Dinapore railway station in here, being four miles from Dinapore itself. It derived its importance from its proximity to Dinapore and from its being on the railway : but it is now suffering like all the considerable towns in the district, from the tendency to make a distributing mart of every railway station, which has been noticed as affecting Patna [James, 1914:8].

The railroad had its Divisional Headquarters here from the beginning; in 1929 two other divisions were closed and incorporated into the Khagaul division, which then became an important rail center. The Railway colony is located north of the tracks in an area separate and distinct from Khagaul, with its own schools, churches, hospital, and habitations. The workshops of the various departments are individually located in the area. There is one large central office. The high officials live in large houses surrounded by grounds and gardens reminiscent of the best in England.

In order to project backwards in time a market survey, the writer has given population figures for Patna, Dinapore, Khagaul, and Calcutta.[1] The inclusion of the category "Christians" as an index of butter consumption is based upon the assumption that the Christians were the English and other Westerners or if Anglo-Indians, as well they might be, then English-oriented. These were the main customers for milk and especially for butter. Presumably the Christians were the richer people and as such could afford butter.

Milk is abundant everywhere, but still the poor get little

1. Data for these tables have been compiled from Censuses of India (1881-1961), Fane (1942), Hunter (1885), Martin (1838), Thornton (1881).

> of it. The luxury of a daily use of *ghee*, or butter, falls only to the lot of the very highest classes [Dutt, 1884:112].

Of course some Christians were Indians; but on the other hand more than just the English were consuming butter. This is submitted as an index of the market potential. Another index is the number — 3,438 — of milk, butter, and ghee sellers in the town of Calcutta reported in 1881, twenty-four years after the rail-road link between Calcutta and Patna was completed. This number includes men, women, Hindus and Muslims, and is the earliest figure of its kind available. In the tables, "Cities" are those commonly designated as such by contemporary records. Naturally, milk, butter, and ghee were also sold in the suburbs and in the rural areas as well.

Part of the large jump in the population of Calcutta between 1931 and 1941 is the result of the incorporation of the city and the enlargement of the census area. The figures from 1931 and before are for the smallest area which is designated "Calcutta." To go to the other extreme and include the suburbs would be almost to double any figure. This is true of all the population figures.

The figures for Patna may be for Patna City, which is the original site of this capital. Through the years the city has crept about eight miles westward, to what used to be known only as Bankipur. The later figures are for the new area.

The "Christians" listed in the Khagaul population probably were the English (and perhaps the Anglo-Indians) who ran the rail-road division. In 1951 the government census made a separate count of the railroad employees. These figures are included in the total for Khagaul, as are those for "Christians."

With the arrival of the railroad, the Cantonment (including Dinapore, of course), Patna, Khagaul, and Calcutta became increasingly important as centers for the sale of milk, butter, ghee, and curd. As will become evident from the history of the Roy family, the Cantonment and Khagaul achieved added importance when milk was converted there into butter.

Until the middle of the nineteenth century, when they first appeared in the village, the Gowāllās, an impoverished caste, followed their traditional occupation of herding and milking, using the marginally productive lands of the diara for grazing. Milk products, bartered and sold in local markets integrated with important regional markets, provided their principal means of subsistence. Through family and friends, by means of batai or "advance money," and frequently by stealing, dairy cattle were acquired. In addition to grazing, diara lands occupied by the Gowāllās were also turned to tillage as an adjunct to their economy, fertile lands being out of their reach. Their low caste status was congruent with their poverty.

As in most of north India, the marriage rule in the predominantly one-caste Gowāllā communities populating the diara was village exogamy; the result of following this rule was the growth of a network of gyno-affiliated relatives in surrounding villages. When it was to their mutual advantage, one of these families "called" relatives from another village to live with them. In this manner kinship provided a route for migration to familiar places.

If mobility be a prime requisite for improving one's economic condition (Moore, 1964:71), then the Gowāllās were ready to move, having neither proprietorship in fields, nor *jajmani** relationships to hold them. And when, with vast numbers of other Indians, they looked for land to plow, their extensive family connections and frequent visitings furnished them with eyes to see new places and envision better positions in society.

Milk products, the prime marketable commodity of the Gowāllās, were, even before the coming of the rail-roads, an important article of commerce though traffic in them was restricted mainly to local and regional markets. Dinapore, located on the diara and a home for many Europeans, was the foremost of the local markets. When the railroad did come to the Patna area in the mid 1800's (about the same time as Phulia Tola was founded), first Patna, then Khagaul displaced Dinapore as the important local market of the district. The railroad made it possible for Calcutta's demand for butter to become an important factor in the economy of Patna District by insuring a steady flow of dairy products from farmer and producer to distributor and consumer. As a result there developed a true price-making market under conditions whereby butter in Calcutta controlled the price of milk in Phulia Tola.

The British also stimulated the demand for butter by their

*Fixed patron-client relationship.

willingness to pay more for it than for ghee (Mukerjee, 1916:95) and by creating in cantonments and railroad colonies a well-paid bureaucracy and work force capable of indulging in English ways. After the British systematically introduced the custom of drinking tea, and drinking it with milk, the demand for milk rose. By 1931 tea drinking had become a national habit :

> There is complete unanimity of opinion regarding the rapid development of the tea-drinking habit in every grade of society, and this is probably the outstanding feature of the period, so far as questions of food and drink are concerned [Lacy, 1933:72].

These developments favored the economy of Khagaul and the village.

Since the British introduced changes in the pattern of Indian life, the temptation is to talk in terms of new elements versus old. But the changes in the case of Phulia Tola were quantitative, not qualitative. The markets, the products, the producers, and the routes which already existed when the railroads came simply entered a period of expansion. The effect of British rule was to widen and deepen existing social and economic patterns, to give a new physical mobility through the railroads and, most important, to give a new political stability to India.

PATNA MUNICIPAL AREA

Year	*Total Population*	*Christians*
1857	284,132	——
1872	158,900	502
1881	170,654	492
1891	165,192	541
1901	134,785	683
1911	136,153	700
1921	119,976	1,274
1931	159,690	1,570
1941	196,415	——
1951	283,479	——
1961	364,594	——

DINAPORE

<table>
<tr><th>Year</th><th>Town</th><th>Cantonment</th><th>Christians</th></tr>
<tr><td>1807</td><td>—</td><td>16,130</td><td>—</td></tr>
<tr><td>1872</td><td>27,914</td><td>14,170</td><td>—</td></tr>
<tr><td>1881</td><td colspan="2">37,893</td><td>1,680</td></tr>
<tr><td>1891</td><td colspan="2">44,419</td><td>1,491</td></tr>
<tr><td>1901</td><td>22,858</td><td>10,841</td><td>1,019</td></tr>
<tr><td>1911</td><td>21,066</td><td>9,959</td><td>1,034</td></tr>
<tr><td>1921</td><td>21,667</td><td>9,210</td><td>1,087</td></tr>
<tr><td>1931</td><td>24,221</td><td>10,217</td><td>17</td></tr>
<tr><td>1941</td><td>30,321</td><td>9,736</td><td>—</td></tr>
<tr><td>1951</td><td>29,170</td><td>13,514</td><td>—</td></tr>
<tr><td>1961</td><td>35,159</td><td>15,058</td><td>—</td></tr>
</table>

CALCUTTA MUNICIPAL AREA

Year	*Total Population*	*Christians*
1872	447,601	21,356
1881	443,219	26,430
1891	649,401	26,406
1901	810,251	33,539
1911	896,067	39,551
1921	907,851	42,212
1931	1,193,651	46,101
1941	2,167,485	—
1951	2,698,494	—
1961	2,927,289	—

KHAGAUL

1872	5,257	214
1881	14,075	307
1891	—	—
1901	8,126	77
1911	6,015	473
1921	7,195	453
1931	7,412	490

		Rail-road
1941	8,795	——
1951	15,748	6,975
1961	20,549	8,322

SIMPLIFIED GENEALOGY OF ROY FAMILY

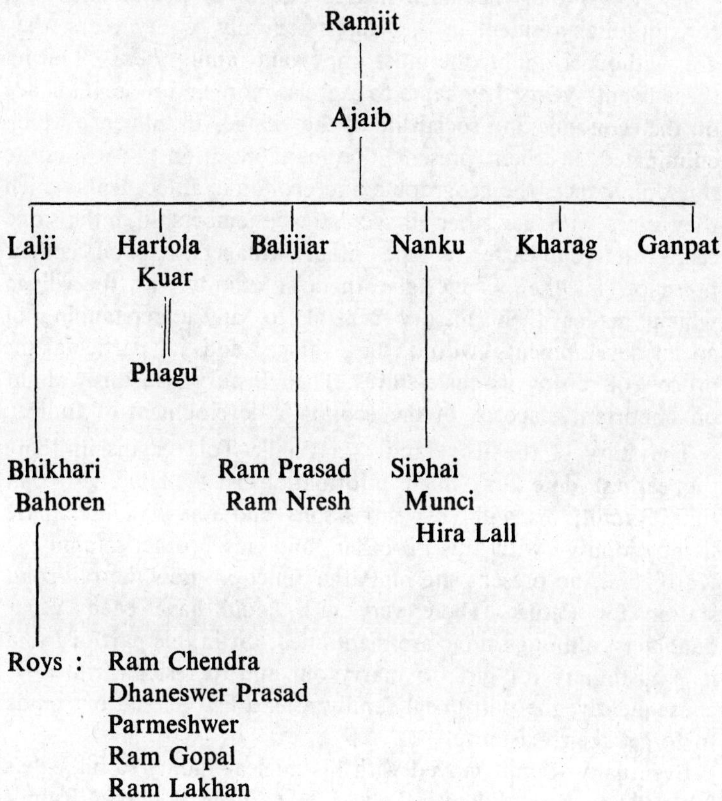

Chapter III

THE ROYS : A HISTORY OF AN ENTREPRENEURIAL FAMILY

The Roy Family has been singled out for particular attention, for, although resident in the village for only twenty years, they are, without a doubt, the most important family there. During these twenty years they came to exercise more and more influence on the economic and social life of the village, an influence which culminated in their present dominant position. Yet despite this dominance, the geographic and economic antecedents which they share with the other villagers, their membership in the same caste and sub-caste as the other villagers, as well as their presence in the village give them an affinity with the village which makes their history central to any understanding of social developments within the village, and in particular the process of raising its caste status. Their history also throws light on important aspects of the economic development of India.[1]

The story of the Roy family of Phulia Tola begins in 1850, the earliest date for which information is available. At that time Ramjit, his wife, his three sons and one daughter were living jointly with his brother and his brother's family at Karbighia, the present site of Patna Junction, now the rail-road station for Patna. There very well could have been other daughters, although none are mentioned, for in this part of India it is customary for girls to marry out and to reside virilocally; consequently, the patrilineal family after a few generations tends to forget their existence.

Eventually Ramjit moved with his nuclear family to his wife's father's house at Nilkanth Tola. It has been said that Ramjit gave his share of the property to his brother and moved to Nilkanth Tola because milk and ghee were plentiful there. It is fruitless to speculate about the specific conditions at Karbighia which prompted Ramjit to leave, but it is true that for a poor

1. Much of the material in this chapter has appeared previously (Swartsberg, 1967).

man Nilkanth Tola was a good place in which to settle, and Ramjit, it is agreed, was poor.

Ramjit did not get any land from his father-in-law, who had sons of his own as heirs. The first son of Ramjit was Ajaib. His last name was Rowt, his caste was Gowāllā. The people of the diara lands had the last name of Rowt while south of there they were known as Gop. Later on, as the caste became more prosperous, the names, or titles as the Indians say, changed, as did the caste name itself.

Ajaib had five sons : Lalji, Balijiar, Nanku, Kharag, and Ganpat. The writer is not sure between which two boys the daughter, Hartola Kuar, was born; but he does know that she was older than Ganpat. Ajaib lived around 1810.

Lalji had two sons — Bhikhari and Bahoren — and a daughter. It was these two sons who eventually moved to Khagaul and became the proprietors of the present Yadava Dairy there. Balijiar had two sons : Ram Prasad and Ram Nresh. Today Ram Nresh is a little over sixty years old and lives in the vicinity of Nilkanth Tola. Nanku had three sons : Siphai, Munci, and Hira Lall. There was also a daughter. Hira Lall, who also must be around sixty, supplied much of the information included in this study. His older brother, Munci, is also alive but is thought to be somewhat senile, especially after he bought an elephant only to display his wealth. Bhikhari and Bahoren died a few years ago, but their five sons are all in good health and contributed to the story, as did Ram Nresh, Balijiar's living son, who visits the Roys frequently.

Kharag had only a daughter, and none of Ganpat's children survived.

Around 1850 the five brothers were living jointly on three acres which they farmed on a sharecropping basis. They also kept animals and sold milk and butter. The family was poor, "damn poor," Hira Lall, Nanku's son, told the writer.* Dhaneshwer Prasad, grandson of Lalji, thus explained the reason why some members of the family left Nilkanth Tola :

> Little land and more mouths to eat there. ... At that time there was no money enough; had there been enough

* Said in English.

money, why they migrate to Dinapore ? How will share if there is little land, and what will the share do ?*

One of the two important events which was to shape the lives of the family occurred around 1885; the daughter, Hartola Kuar, was married to Phagu Bhagat, Butterman of Khagaul (as he is designated in a document). The other event, which took place a few years later, was the marriage of Nanku Rowt to a girl from Nya Tola, just next to the Cantonment at Dinapore.

Phagu Bhagat and his "brother" (agnates of the same generation being referred to as brothers), Lachman Bhagat, had originally come from the Cantonment area also. They were about the same age (though not of the same generation) and related — so that people spoke of them as brothers. Actually, Phagu's father's father's brother's son's son's son was Lachman Bhagat. The important thing is that they were in the same patriline and they knew each other well. At one time they may have lived together and been in business together. Lachman had two sons, one of whom is Deoki Nandan of whom mention will be made later. Phagu and Hartola Kuar had children, but non survived infancy.

Of the two brothers, Lachman is by far the richer. At the time of his death, around 1910, he had at least thirty-six acres in the vicinity of Phulia Tola, a mile south of Khagaul, and another 300 to 600 acres in the vicinity of the Cantonment, the number depending upon who is telling the story. He owned a large, ornate house in Khagaul as well as another on his property in Phulia Tola. People still talk about his wealth, how he carried his money in sacks, how he used to come into Khagaul from Dinapore on his own pony cart. By the standards of Khagaul, he was an aristocrat and man of wealth. In fact, he commanded not less respect than the zamindars (landlords) of the Badalpura estate of Khagaul, according to Hartola Kuar's great-nephew.

Lachman made his money by buying and selling milk and butter and shipping it to Calcutta, where the price was two and a half times what it was locally. The East India Company was his best customer. At Calcutta he maintained his own

*Said in English.

establishment for selling to retailers. When the writer asked why Lachman went into business, his informant replied, "Anyone look after anything profitable."* The fact is that Lachman exploited the opportunities afforded by the coming of the railroad to the fullest. By all accounts he was the first to send butter to Calcutta from the Khagaul area, and he set a pattern of trade which continues to this day.

An observer in 1916 commented that the great demand for butter had made it a very profitable commodity while the demand for ghee was declining (Mukerjee, 1916:92 ff.). It actually costs less to make butter than ghee.

Lachman and Phagu had first come to Khagaul in search of suppliers of milk. From time to time the supply from one locality dwindles because the grazing is not so good, or the cattle die of disease or simply dry up during the hot season, while in another area the supply of milk improves. Collecting stations are forever springing up and fading away. At the time mentioned there were large herds south of Khagaul with plenty of open land to accommodate them.

Although not nearly as rich as Lachman, Phagu was well off by the standards of his wife's family, for he owned a few houses and a few acres in Phulia Tola. He had a butter shop where he sold to the Europeans and to Lachman Bhagat. Hartola Kuar, as the wife of a man of moderate means, was not in purdah; in her home at Nilkanth Tola she had worked in the fields. The writer was discussing with Dhaneshwer Prasad, the second oldest of the brothers of the present Roy family, the origin of the purdah in his family. The two of them were trying to date it by reference to relatives alive at the time. There was some confusion in the writer's mind; Dhaneshwer quickly resolved it : "When the income increases, they [women] prohibited to work in the fields."*

Another clue to Phagu's relatively high status is his last name, Bhagat. Having come originally from north of Khagaul, he might have started out life with the name Rowt, as did Hartola Kuar's family. Bhagat was a respected name (literally it means "follower of God") which was taken by those among the Gowāllās

*Said in English.

who had become educated and achieved success. In Phulia Tola, and possibly in the vicinity of Khagaul, the Gowāllās had the name Gop, meaning "herder". Lachman is always Lachman Bhagat; Phagu is Phagu Bhagat, except sometimes when a clerk slips and writes Phagu Gop.

My hosts, the Roy family, the lineal descendants of Ajaib and Lalji, used to argue with me that the names on the documents were not always of their own choosing, that the clerks would write down whatever names they pleased. Actually these names were their old family-caste appellations which they were in the process of discarding, but by which they were still known in public. The clerks were simply reflecting the traditional resistance to changes in the family names of those who, like the Roys, were with their rising economic status seeking a corresponding elevation in social status. When Hartola Kuar's brother's sons Bhikhari and Bahoren — after having lived in Khagaul for some time and become known as Bhagat — went back to Nilkanth Tola to execute a document, they found their family name still recorded as Rowt, for in the old neighborhood they continued to be known as such.

The writer has hesitated to use the word *dairy* to describe the milk, butter, and ghee business, for it calls to mind a fair-sized establishment with many employees and gleaming machinery which turns out many products, all neatly wrapped and packaged. Such was and is not the case. The words *shop* or *stall* would be better descriptions, for these enterprises were small, employing few men. At the time we are speaking of, milk was made into curd first, for there was no means of separating the cream from the milk; then the butter was made in wooden, hand-operated churns. Nothing was packaged; it was all put into large earthen or metal jars. At one time Phagu operated out of the ground floor of his house. This was the usual practice then and today.

In fact, from a short official health report written in the late 1800's complaining about the unsanitary conditions, it is apparent the old section of Khagaul has not changed much. It is the typical bazaar town of a few narrow streets of hard-packed dirt or cobblestones, of open shops piled with goods in crowded quarters. The shops which occupy the ground floors of two- or three-story buildings are really open verandahs, boarded up at night. Goats and mangy dogs roam and eat garbage that has been thrown into the street. People stop at shops and at tea stalls as they jostle one another in a steady stream from morning until night, amid hectic activity and endless conversation. The shouts from the driver of an oxcart squeezing its way through an indifferent swirl of people mingle with the dust and the odors.

In the bazaar the changes most apparent to eye and ear are those brought about by the installation of electricity in 1938; now the bright clear bulbs, hanging bare by their cords in every shop, and the constant blare of recorded movie music give a gay carnival air to the market. Another change, important in the context of this paper, is the greater number of tea stalls on the main streets. These are centers for meeting and gossiping, as people sit around tables inside or squat in the street in front of the stall.

The most notable changes are in the section just north of the railroad tracks, on the station side. Here the scene is more orderly, with wide streets lined with offices, quarters, and various other buildings belonging to the railroad. Here are the railroad hospital, the railroad cinema and club, the churches (attended by few since the British left), and the railroad schools. These last are supposed to be for the children of railroad personnel.

As the figures indicate, the Railway colony has steadily grown; its employees as a group have always earned the highest wages in the area.

Phulia Tola, Khagaul, and Dinapore are on the northern end of the centuries-old Sher Shah Road.

Hartola Kuar was a generous, affectionate person; she periodically visited her family at Nilkanth Tola, a distance of fifteen miles as the roads go; but more often she was visited by her family, and especially by her youngest brother, Ganpat, who spent more and more time in Khagaul. He helped take care of Phagu's animals, worked in Phagu's fields, and lent Phagu a hand in the milk business. Often he was the one who delivered the milk to the Sahibs. Between times his sister taught him to read and write, just as she had been taught by a tutor employed by Phagu. They were the first in the family to become literate.

A few years after Hartola Kuar married, her brother Nanku Rowt married a girl from Nya Tola, next to Dinapore Cantonment. Shortly afterwards Nanku's father-in-law invited him to come and live with him and become heir to his few acres of land, for the father-in-law had no male issue. (Land you may own is better than land you only sharecrop, especially when the land grows sweet rice rather than hard corn). Moreover, arguments had broken out among the women. So Nanku left Nilkanth Tola and never returned except to visit.

Men always attribute the separation of a family to fights among women, and to some extent these are indeed a cause for separation, for the women come from different villages and different families. But this is not always the reason the joint family separates, as the men would have you believe. More often there is an economic cause, as this history will demonstrate. (For contrasting views of this problem see Bailey, 1957:92; Epstein, 1962:176 ff., 306, 302; Rosenfeld, 1958:1127-1139; and Harper, 1958:94-96; Klass, 1961:131-132.)

When Nanku moved to Nya Tola, Siphai, his first son, had already been born, a fact which would date the move to about 1890. His other two sons, Munci and Hira Lall, were born at Nya Tola.

By 1885, when he was about eighteen years old, Ganpat was working full time for Phagu, his brother-in-law. In India brothers-in-law have a special relationship to each other; they are supposed to be close to one another and are most likely to call upon each other in time of trouble. Siphai, who was younger, had taken Ganpat's place; now it was Siphai who was visiting his father's sister, Hartola Kuar, more and more and staying longer and longer, eating the sweets of the sweet shops, tasting the excitement of Khagaul, until he too became a member of Phagu's family. As Ganpat before him, Siphai did everything; he did farm work, watched the animals, took care of chores in the butter shop and even found time to go to lower elementary school.

Phagu died when still a young man, perhaps forty years old, and he left a young widow just under thirty years of age. The time was 1898. Ganpat took charge of the family in Khagaul along with Phagu's shop and other property; it was assumed Ganpat or some men of the widow's family would do so. Anywhere in the world it can be awkward for a woman not to have a man in her house, be it husband or some blood relative; it is especially so in India, where a woman needs a man to protect her. As an upper-class woman, Hartola Kuar was in purdah. Usually she remained in the house, and if she left it, some man in her family would accompany her. Not until 1937 did women get the legal right to inherit. Even today in the village this law is not observed — unless you know someone acquainted with the law and can get it enforced. Traditional law says that when a woman's husband dies, his property shall go equally to his sons and, if there are no sons, to his brothers. But the widow must be fed and clothed. If she has no sons or only young sons, her husband's brothers may try to force her out of the house, for they in turn fear the widow will come under the influence of her patriline and assert a claim on the land or the crops although such a claim could only be enforced if she had sons. James reports "the very common case where a Hindu widow alienates, land to her own relations, ostensibly for consideration and for necessity, and the transfer is questioned by the family of the deceased husband [1914:120]."

There are cases reported of men, each of whom, wishing to protect his wife from his own brothers, puts property in his wife's name. Such was the case with Hartola Kuar. Since women have had the right to inherit, the conflict between a woman's *naiher* (parents' house) and her husband's brothers has become more evident. Now the woman's father and brothers may try to persuade her to come live with them after her husband's death in order to sell his share of the land. This makes the unprotected woman a likely seller of land below market price. Her house will be pervaded by an air of mutual distrust and hostility. Petty jealousies will be fanned anew; her brothers will tug at her, and someone with an interest in buying the land will incite her. So at last she will sell the land.

One man put it in personal terms :

> Yes, if it's [land] worth R. 10,000, you'll get it for R. 4,000 or Rs. 5,000. They [widows] think that nobody is taking care of her, so what's the use of keeping it ? What can she do if God doesn't help her. If there's a woman and her husband and children are dead, there is nobody to take care of her. How can anybody take care of her as well [as her husband] ? She won't listen; she doesn't know [the price].*

*Translated from Hindi.

She will have to sell it cheaply, for her market will be limited to those who have land in the vicinity (or who have relatives with land close by), for land must be worked to have value, and only those who live within a radius of a few miles will be able to work it. Indians say, "The sandy land which is near your house is gold, but the gold which is far away from your house is sand." Moreover, she will have to sell it to a rich, powerful family. Those words are synonymous. Knowing the fight which is brewing, only a powerful family will want to buy it, for the land will have to be defended by force or in court. Thereafter she will sell the land cheaply, her market being limited by geography and social class.

Disputes over land are the most common cause of conflict in India. Every ethnographer notes this; local newspapers in India carry stories daily about group clashes over land; land litigation accounts for the majority of court cases. Since the establishment of the British court system, the writer's guess is that there has been a decline in the resort to physical force. Two sayings he heard repeatedly were : "Might makes right"; and, "if you have a wife, money, or land, you are going to have a fight."*

The practice of selling to rich people land which is in dispute is not limited to widows. Ram Chendra Roy, the oldest member of the writer's host's family, explained : "Might makes right. If someone encroaches on land for some time and the other does nothing, but when the land is sold to a strong man, he will take back his land by force."* And Ram Chendra ought to know, for in this time he had been such a strong man.

The poor man figures he will lose the land in the long run; better at least to get some money for it.

To get back to our story. Balijiar came down to Khagaul around 1900 with his oldest son, Ram Presad, to give a hand. Hartola Kuar was delighted to have her family with her. Deoki Nandan Bhagat, who, like his father, Lachman Bhagat, was in the butter business, had claimed her property; as long as her family remained with her, however, he was unable to enforce his claim; she was "safe".

Although business slowly improved for the family at Khagaul, not all went smoothly; Ram Prasad died, and Siphai had a

* Translated from Hindi.

fight with Ganpat. Siphai accused Ganpat of giving the customers short weight, with the result that Siphai left to rejoin his father at Nya Tola, near the Cantonment. This loss of personnel (Balijiar was still with Ganpat) was made good by the two sons of Lalji (the oldest of the five brothers) — Bhikhari and Bahoren. Lalji was left at the head of the remaining joint family in Nilkanth Tola, now made up of his wife, his brother Kharag and his family, and the wives and children of the men who were in Khagaul, as well as people of the older generation and their descendants. The men in Khagaul were constantly going to and from Nilkanth Tola; the women had no reason to be in Khagaul; they were needed in Nilkanth Tola to look after household duties, work in the fields, and take care of the animals and children. Furthermore, there the women had all their friends and neighbors — all of the same caste, and the majority of the same sub-caste. In the planting and harvesting season, those who could be spared from business went to Nilkanth Tola to assist in the work.

Business in town was not confined to milk, butter and ghee. Money lending was a profitable source of income, and every merchant, regardless of caste, had his hand in it. Risk was minimal, for most loans were secured by mortgages on land. The man who lent the money had the use of the land until the debt on it was repaid. He had the choice of plowing the land himself or putting it out on batai (half-and-half sharecropping). By 1910 Ganpat and Bhikhari and Bahoren owned four and a half acres in Phulia Tola, most of it by converting mortgages into sales. When the mortgagor was pressed to borrow more money — to pay for a wedding, funeral, or the expenses of some illness — Ganpat would give the money to the mortgagor only on condition that the land be sold outright to Ganpat at a price below its market value. (Customarily land is mortgaged at half its value).

While Hartola Kuar's brothers and nephews had left the diara lands of Nilkanth Tola only a few years back, they were learning fast. They had seen Lachman Bhagat become one of the richest men around, and Lachman was of their same caste, sub-caste, and a distant relative as well. Lachman was a customer of theirs, too. It must have been at this time that the family's business principle was first enunciated : money should be like a stream, always flowing.

Balijiar decided around 1900 to go into business for himself; he left Khagaul and travelled to Marwan in Muzaffarpur district, north of the Ganges. In business there was Badri Bhagat, also a Gowāllā from Nilkanth Tola, who supposedly was earning R. 1000 a year selling butter to Calcutta. There too in the butter business were Badri's brother Gopi and Bamanan Bhagat, all of whom Balijiar's family had sold to at one time or other. To Balijiar the milk and butter business certainly seemed easier and more profitable than farming on the sandy land of the diara. After two years Balijiar called for Siphai to join him, for he felt Siphai was an experienced man, having worked for Ganpat in Khagaul. Siphai left Dinapore, where he had been with his father, Nanku, but disagreements broke out between Siphai and Balijiar, and business was bad anyway. Siphai claimed he was not getting fed well enough. They went their separate ways — Balijiar to Nilkanth Tola, disgusted with business; Siphai to Nya Tola, with a taste for business. When Siphai confided to his mother that he wanted to go into the butter business for himself, she gave him the R. 50, that she had put aside as her own money from selling milk, to provide the small amount of equipment necessary to pay the monthly rent of R. 4 on a shop near the present bus stand.

The butter merchants in the area had a two-part problem : to find suppliers of milk and then to convert the milk into butter in sufficient quantities to make the selling profitable. The supply was variable and the manufacturing process slow; consequently many businesses were short lived. The Military Cantonment had its own dairy; and even though it made butter only for its own personnel, it had to supplement its supplies from the stocks of local shopkeepers.

To get milk Siphai went back to his own neighborhood, the diara lands, as did Chandraman Bhagat who was also in business in the Cantonment Area and had bought milk and butter from Siphai's family in the past. It was a small world of Gowāllā butter merchants who circulated, combined, split, recombined wherever milk could be collected and butter made, and sold to the local sahibs. Something was about to happen to upset this balance.

In 1908 the military dairy installed a mechanical cream separator; at about the same time another butter merchant, Mongel Bhagat, also a Gowāllā, got a cream separator, as did eventually the other three merchants. The mechanical separator, though operated by hand, accelerated the process of manufacturing butter, for no longer was it necessary to make curd first : the separator made the cream quickly available for direct conversion into butter. Production was increased more than tenfold. Even the leftover milk was sold.

As soon as he heard about the separator, Siphai realized its possibilities and ordered a machine from Calcutta. He took the machine to Jahanabad on the Patna-Gaya railroad line, a distance of twenty-seven miles south of Patna, where he set up a collecting station and hired a man to run it. Milk was available there. Unfortunately, the man stole the machine and ran away.

It should be noted that this collecting station, as well as others mentioned in this paper, is on or nearby the railroad line.

The loss of his machine did not deter Siphai; he borrowed more money from his mother, who had to pawn her ornaments for this purpose, and took the train to Aligarh (U.P.) to sce Edward Keventer, and English importer of the Alpha Cream Separators manufactured in Sweden. (The Edward Keventer Company also produced butter there and in Simla and Darjeeling. The company continues in business today.)

Siphai bought a larger machine than the first one and obtained a distributorship for the machine from Keventer with the understanding that Siphai would sell the machine at a 15 per cent commission. Actually, Siphai sold them at 100 per cent markup.

With increased production from the machines, and with the sales of the machines themselves contributing to more than half his income, Siphai within a short period of time was doing well. In October 1910, he officially named the business the Siphai Bhagat Dairy (written in English). At this time a former inhabitant of Nilkanth Tola was selling Siphai's butter in Calcutta for a commission of R. 1 per earthen jar, and Siphai was making a gross profit of R. 10 per jar, compared to a maximum of R. 15 per day before the introduction of the machine. With the profits Siphai bought land and built a new dairy in 1918 at a cost of R. 4,000. Siphai Bhagat had learned how to convert milk into a stream of rupees. O'Malley, writing in 1907, may have had him or Lachman in mind when he described "some Goalas round Dinapore who had made small fortunes in the butter trade [1906:65]." When he started in business the family had two or three acres in Nya Tola; in 1949, when they had almost 200 acres, the Siphai Bhagat family stopped buying land. "We bought land from the profits, not from the capital,"* Hira Lall, Siphai's youngest brother, explained to the writer. By this he meant that a certain amount of money had been set aside for the business; the remainder was used to buy land. When they stopped buying farm land in 1949, they bought income properties in Ashok Market, Patna. In 1957 they left the dairy business because of trouble with the government over back taxes, because new regulations in Calcutta called for more fat content in the butter, because of import restrictions on cream separators, and, finally, because the younger generation was not interested in continuing the business. In 1957 they built instead a cold storage warehouse for perishable foods near the old dairy in Dinapore. The younger generation initiated the new cold storage business.

Siphai did not do all this alone; with him he had Ram Dass, a fellow villager from Nya Tola who became his manager; and later on Siphai's brothers, Munci and Hira Lall, joined him in the business. The writer has been told it was really Ram Dass's idea to go to Aligarh to get the distributorship for the separator. In fact, Ram Dass is said to have tried to get the machine directly from Sweden. After the dairy started to make money, a disagreement arose between Siphai and Ram Dass. Ram Dass had thought he was a partner, but Siphai informed him he was a manager, nothing more. Ram Dass left.

To resume the story of the family at Khagaul. Ganpat and his brother's two sons — Bhikhari and Bahoren — bought a cream separator some time after Siphai's purchase. They either bought it from him or ordered it from Calcutta where they had connections with a Bengali butter merchant. This happened a long time ago, and it is difficult to establish the true facts, especially when each branch of the family wants to take full credit for the transaction.

At one time the Khagaul branch of the family did sell

---

* Translated from Hindi.

separators for Siphai Bhagat. Mital Bhagat, Sheo Pradad Bhagat, Mithajit Bhagat had acquired separators at about the same time as Bhikhari and Bahoren. They were all Gowāllās and in the Cantonment region, and shipping butter to Calcutta. In 1914 the two branches of the family went into partnership, at various times in Samastipur and in Muzaffarpur districts, depending upon the supply of milk available. These districts being near the rail-road, the butter was shipped directly to Calcutta. This partnership, which applied only for the collecting stations, lasted on and off until 1937 when an argument over the sharing of profits broke it up.

By the beginning of World War I, Ganpat and Bhikhari and Bahoren Bhagat were in charge of the butter shop. Business had improved; more and more Indians were eating butter locally; more and more butter was being sent by overnight train to Calcutta where it was sold by a Bengali agent. In 1918 they officially became a business, meaning they had to pay taxes to Khagaul. They were busy men — taking care of the dairy, seeing the family at Nilkanth Tola, and walking the dirt road to Phulia Tola to take care of their fields. Some day in the future they would hire men to do the farming. (People would whisper to the writer that they remembered Bhikhari and Bahoren when they did their own plowing and harvesting.)

All agree that the hot-tempered Bahoren was the smart one; probably it is he who thought of extending to his milk suppliers the old practice of "advance money." Bahoren did not own cows — because of their low and uncertain productivity — and therefore, could guarantee a steady supply of milk only by financing the herdsmen who supplied him. Loans to them were usually made without collateral, but he was well paid for any risks he took. The herdsman was required to repay his loans in milk at below-market prices. Moreover, the herdsman was likely to need money from time to time to pay the expenses of some special occasion, such as a wedding, and Bahoren would advance the sum under the same conditions of repayment. In such a situation a mutual dependency exists; each party gains : the herdsman, a source of ready cash; the butter merchant, a regular supply of milk at a reduced price.

In 1918 Bahoren had a row with Ganpat and ran away. He was twenty-three years old, married, and the father of two children. His own father was looking after the family at Nilkanth Tola. Nobody had heard from him for a week. Then news came back : Bahoren was living with the agent for Siphai at Calcutta. Ganpat went to Calcutta to ask Bahoren to return; Bahoren refused; he suggested to Ganpat that instead of returning he, Bahoren, stay on at Calcutta and sell butter for both Siphai and themselves. Ganpat went home, asked Siphai's opinion, and Siphai agreed.

This arrangement set the pattern for a division of family labor that is followed to this day — one man at Calcutta; one man in the shop at Khagaul; and one man, the oldest, in charge of agricultural lands. This pattern was also followed by the Siphai Bhagat branch. As long as everything went well, the two families would take turns in sending men to Calcutta. When the Calcutta partnership broke up, each family had to station a man there; the practice of alternating men at Calcutta, however, continued within each family. The one who came back from Calcutta would be technically off duty; he would attend to such family duties as escorting women, representing the family at weddings or funerals if the others were too busy, attending to the collecting stations, or going to court. Often he would just hang around the dairy.

The years between the wars were ones of slow, steady growth for the Bhagats (as they were now called) of Khagaul. Following Ganpat's example, they decided to buy land at Phulia Tola, for here the fertile land was suited to the cultivation of the staple of the Indian diet, rice, as well as other crops. They erected a mud hut for sleeping overnight and set up cattle pens.

Some of the people at Phulia Tola they knew already, for they had relatives at Nilkanth Tola; the others they quickly became acquainted with, for like themselves they were all Gowāllās and Krishnauts. One family they especially became friendly with was Nand Lall's, a part of the *Mahato* (headmen) family, the original settlers of the village. Often they ate with Nand Lall. And Nand Lall and some of the others of Phulia Tola celebrated weddings at the house of the Bhagats. Near the end of the period, Nand Lall started plowing some of the Bhagats' land on batai basis.

The Gowāllās in Phulia Tola and in surrounding villages were an asset to the Bhagat family of Khagaul. They formed the most numerous caste in Bihar and had a reputation for being stupid, uncouth, and easily provoked to fighting. At least twice a day the Gowāllās were in the market place selling their milk, or at their favorite, hangout, Bhikhari Bhagat's shop. At times when the Bhagats needed help, their castemen were there with a show of strength. By now the Bhagats had a reputation which made the other businessmen of Khagaul afraid of them; for they had taken over small pieces of adjoining property and were quick to go to court. Bhikhari and Bahoren had learned about courts when they tried to collect money from debtors. A man in Khagaul explained : "What could we do ? We were afraid; we were afraid of the rich man when he walled off the street. A rich man can make it all mixed up [establish a false case]. I would have to spend money. What could I do ? People should be afraid of a rich man."*

People live close together in India, whether in town or in village; frictions develop. The Bhagats had many disputes with their Muslim neighbors on both sides of them.

The Bhagats used various tactics to acquire land. The writer has already outlined that used in buying from a widow. Another tactic was connected with their money-lending business. They would allow small amounts to mount up to a sizable sum and then present the account for payment. The debtor, having kept no records and unable either to contest or to pay off the debt, could only accede to Bahoren's "suggestion" to settle the debt for a conveyance of land. Another way to get land — and cheaply at that — was to buy it from a Religious Trust. Such lands, supposedly held in perpetuity by religious organizations, were managed, by *pandits* (priests) who represented themselves as proprietors. Since their titles were no clear, the properties might be bought from these priests at prices below their market value. Additional opportunities to purchase land — again at low prices — also arose. At that time many Muslims fled the area, leaving their properties in the hands of relatives. Some of these would presume full ownership and sell the properties cheaply because of the risks to the purchaser in acquiring land without a clear title.

As men of power and wealth, the Bhagats were often sought

---

* Translated literally from Hindi.

after. A weak man whose land was being encroached upon by a strong man would sell to the Bhagats; people who wanted to mortgage land or borrow money came to Bhikhari's shop, for the Bhagats were always ready to listen to a proposition. From 1928 to 1936 they had Mahadeo Bhagat, a Gowāllā from a village just south of Phulia Tola, managing the buying and selling of lands for them. He left after an argument over money. A man who had fought them in the village told the writer : "Whatever money they have earned was not earned in the right way. Whatever it says on the paper, the people didn't get that much. They had the sale deed made by force."* What the Bhagats were doing others were doing too; the Bhagats were merely doing it more often. It was the way of the market.

The shop, just off the main street of Khagaul, where a constant stream of people passed, became a hangout for friends, relatives, and villagers. The benches under the verandah have been worn into shiny grooves by the numerous visitors who sat there to pass the time of day with Bhikhari and Bahoren, and (later on) their children — Ram Chendra, Dhaneshwer Prasad, Parmeshwer, Ram Gopal, and Ram Lakhan. Twice a week the heads of the two branches of the family would meet there; and the custom continues today.

During this period Hartola Kuar had turned over all her property to Bhikhari and Bahoren. Ganpat had died in the 1920's. The dispute with her husband's relation, Deoki Nandan, had finally been settled in 1933. The family in Nilkanth Tola was being taken care of. At every harvest the ox cart would carry produce to the old village. Additional land was purchased there, and the earthen-walled house was replaced with one of brick walls and a tiled roof.

The next part of the story concerns the move of the family from Khagaul to the village of Phulia Tola in 1946. From the earliest days the family had a mud hut — next to the dirt road — where men could sleep over if necessary. As the Roys (their name today) bought more land in the village it became apparent that a move to the village near their land would eventually have to be made. The family, it is true, was growing and needed room, relations with their Muslim neighbors were troubled,

* Translated from Hindi.

and a village was considered to be a better place to raise children than dirty, crowded Khagaul. But their main reason was the necessity to maintain closer supervision over the lands which they owned. Just as it was logical to buy land in a village close to Khagaul and the home of their own sub-caste, was it logical that they establish their residence there. Land must be watched, taken care of. A foreman will steal from you and other villagers will cut your crop, graze their cattle on your land, even plow your land and literally steal it by moving the boundary wall between plots. Or they will divert the water irrigating your fields. Lachman Bhagat had employed a foreman and workers, and people had stolen from him, but Lachman was rich and obviously did not care. The Roys were not *that* rich. Up to the time they moved into the village, they had given some of their land on batai to Deo Narain's family, with whom they had kinship relations from Nilkanth Tola and by whom they were now invited into the village. (Again, if you give your lands on batai you have to make sure your tenant is not stealing.)

The Roys had not planned to move for a few months, but the Muslim-Hindu riots were taking place, and, though no riots occurred in Khagaul, the town was tense and the Roys nervous, especially when on both sides of them lived Muslim neighbors with whom they had been involved in arguments and litigation. The ground floor of their new house in the village was not fully completed, and the *puja* (ceremony) which precedes occupancy had not been performed, but the Roys packed hastily and moved in.

The writer has already mentioned that the Roys while they lived in Khagaul had good relationships with the villagers, especially Nand Lall's family. On one occasion when the Roys were having a dispute in Khagaul with a neighbor over the location of a door, the Roys were able to summon the villagers from Phulia Tola for a show of caste strength to back them up.

Aside from any psychological motivations — distance lends enchantment (or as the Indian says : the drums sound sweeter from afar) — there were concrete reasons why friction developed between the Roy family and the village. Phulia Tola is an island of compact dwellings surrounded by fields. The lands not owned by Phulia Tola people were owned by the different castes living in other villages as close as a mile away. (Some land was owned by Gowāllās of other villages, but the problem was the same.) Such landowners could not keep watch on their lands and at the same time were anxious to avoid fights with a unified village of Gowāllās. But Phulia Tola people had gotten used to grazing their animals on other people's land. When the Roys bought much of this land and moved into the village to take it over, conflict developed, for old habits are hard to break. The villagers resented their free grazing land being taken away by the Roys. At first the Roys tried to settle disputes within the village by calling meetings of the *panches* (respected men); the offenders were then admonished and fined, but soon the villagers got tired of punishing themselves, so they did not come to the meetings. Then the Roys went outside the village and turned to the police and the courts for redress. Through a series of incidents, mutual antagonism built up between the two factions, especially between the Roys and the descendants of Nand Lall's family, the family of Deo Narain, the very ones who had invited them into the village.

Until the arrival of the Roys, Deo Narain's family was the richest and most powerful in the village. They were one of a group of families descended from the original founding family (the Mahato — headman — family).

The Roys' house and Deo Narain's house stand side by side, symbolic of the change in power in the village. Deo Narain's is a large flat house composed of two square one-story buildings; it used to be the largest house in the village. It is overshadowed, however, by the Roys' house, a tall two-story structure, white-washed and decorated in blue, and the most imposing building for miles around. From the top floors of the Roys' house you can easily look into the inner courtyard of Deo Narain's house, where the women stay. Naturally, Deo Narain resented such proximity.

The tension between the two families came to a climax one bright December morning in a cane field where a fight almost broke out. Ostensibly the argument was over ownership of the crop which had been cultivated by Deo Narain on land purchased before the harvest by the Roys; actually, it was a fight over prestige, to determine who was the big man of the village. Both sides understood this. The Roys initiated the fight, refused to compromise, and finally won their case in court, where the defendants were all fined, and one man was sentenced to jail for three months. According to village custom Deo Narain was entitled to the entire crop because he had cultivated it. The Roys won the case because they were able to hire better lawyers, bribe witnesses, and silence those who could defend Deo Narain. The entire matter was clarified for the writer by Deo Narain in the following words : "If you have money, nobody will say anything. People know he is a money man; if I fight with him, I can't beat him. They didn't say anything [in my behalf]."*

Since the cane-field fight, the Roy family have consolidated their position, and consequently have never been directly challenged again; their dominant position is acknowledged. Their land holdings are a source of power, as were those of the landlords of old with their jajmani relationships, for about half of the Roys' land is let out to tenants. Since land is scarce, this gives them power over the tenants; a man who needs your land is not likely to make trouble. The family would prefer to rent it all, but in turn the village would then have power over them; instead, they keep a crew of workers and plow half of it themselves.

Their experience in 1949 taught them the danger of being alone in the village. Since then two families, related in different ways to the Roys, have settled in Phulia Tola by the invitation and with the help of the Roys. One other family, a business acquaintance, came in the same way. Two other families were invited but did not want to come.

In addition to bringing people into the village, the Roys, in order to bolster their position, made an alliance with one of the factions already residing in the village. Being rich, the Roys could be helpful in lending money at no interest, giving land out to rent, and getting jobs for people — especially through Ram Gopal, who was a high government official.

The introduction of the government-sponsored Panchayat Raj in Bihar in 1950 further strengthened the Roys' power. The Roys recognized its importance from the very start and always managed to secure for themselves one or both of the important positions in the Panchayat. To this end they have bought votes,

---

* Translated from Hindi.

stuffed ballot boxes, and demonstrated how the friends of a rich family can be rewarded and its enemies punished. Money was always forthcoming for building a community hall, fixing a school, or developing a health clinic, and it all contributed to their prestige.

We will return to Khagaul and take up the story of the Roys' business affairs where we left it — just prior to the outbreak of World War II.

In 1942 the Japanese bombed Calcutta. At that time Dhaneshwer Prasad was taking his regular turn in the shop in Calcutta. The bombing threw the city into turmoil. People fled, Dhaneshwer Prasad stayed. The prices of commodities, including butter, rose. An embargo was placed on incoming goods, but by bribing a rail-road employee the Roys got their butter through. They stopped selling butter in Khagaul; much more money could be made in Calcutta. The money made in Calcutta was eventually used to increase their land holdings in the village.

Up to and including 1941 the Roys had accumulated 16.5 acres in Phulia Tola; the most they had bought in any year until then was 2.7 acres. In 1942 they bought 3.4 acres; by 1964 they had 93 acres under their control, all in and around Phulia Tola. The 1941 figure of 3.4 acres was not a dramatic increase, for by this time land had become scarce; the population increase had had its effect. The Roys had to wait patiently for the opportunities to present themselves. Many other things had happened to the Roy family besides their business success. Let us review them.

When the writer asked Ram Nresh, Balijiar's second son, why Nanku, Siphai's father, did not go into business, he answered, "You can't do business without any education."* Bhikhari and Bahoren knew this well. Dhaneshwer Prasad, Bhikhari's second son, explained : "Our guardians compel all the children to get the study, but those who go up and break their study, that depends on his mind, not guardian's mind."** He made clear the practicality of going to school :

> They get the study only to improve their life ... and to get knowledge, of course. ... When he will study, and after

* Translated from Hindi.

** Said in English.

> learning, he may enter into business; he may enter into service. Or if he wants to cultivate, he may improve the cultivation; that [he] will get from study.*

Education, it may be added, also gives prestige.

Education was a remarkable achievement for the Roys. Consider that Ganpat, Balijiar, Siphai, Bhikhari, and Bahoren were barely literate although Siphai's youngest brother, Hira Lall, went through high school (although he did not graduate). The five sons of Bhikhari and Bahoren all were given an education and one of them, Ram Gopal, graduated with a B. S. degree.

All of Bahoren's sons went to the Railway High School, for it was the best school in Khagaul. All the sons of the present five brothers have been allowed to go as far as their inclination and ability would take them. The girls routinely go to seventh or eighth class, and then get married.

One of the present five brothers, Ram Gopal, who has the B.S., entered the Civil Service and today is Under-secretary of Local Self Government in the Bihar State Government at Patna. After graduating from college, Ram Gopal took a three-months' tour of the European continent at his family's expense. On that tour he negotiated an agency for a Swedish cream separator, but nothing came of the negotiations because the Indian Government shortly afterwards restricted the importation of dairy machinery.

The Roys also advanced themselves socially and in a manner peculiarly Indian. They participated in and were alert to the common efforts of the members of their caste to up-caste themselves. An Indian does not go up or down in the social scale alone or by himself; he is tied to his caste. As his caste's fortunes rise and fall, so do his. (Marginal man is not applicable to Indian caste society; in fact, he who might be such in another culture, becomes a leader within his caste.) The writer once asked an official in the local Yādāvā (formerly Gowāllā) caste movement why he bothered to work so hard to raise the standards of his fellow caste members. "Well," he said, "first comes my close family; then comes my other family — my relatives, and then comes my caste." It was clear that he regarded the members

*Said in English.

of his caste as extensions of his family. Even though the social status of individual families fluctuates it does so within the framework of caste. An individual who climbs economically but whose caste is low in prestige suffers socially.

While "Sanskritization and Westernization are linked processes in modern India and it is not possible to understand one without reference to the other [Srinivas, 1962:9]," it is possible to distinguish these two elements in upcasting and, in the case of the Gowāllās of the area under review, to discern the shift in emphasis among them :

> In South Bihar the Goala movement has been less in the direction of advancing caste claim to wear the sacred thread and so forth and more towards social reform [Tallents, 1923:23].

Around 1940 the movement split over the question whether religious or social aims should predominate in upcasting. In the national conference the writer attended in 1965, ritual was ignored and education was emphasized. While the village is nominally vegetarian and wears the genu (sacred thread), the younger men have little interest in these things. The Roys paid attention to both education and ritual. In the early 1920's both branches of the family adopted vegetarianism, education, purdah, and the genu. They remain faithful to all four to the present day.[1]

Small, local caste conferences as early as 1912 preached the above four points, among others (Anon., 1912:274). These conferences continue to the present day, but their present emphasis is on education and political unity. During the writer's stay in India he attended a local and a national caste conference. History amply documents the persistent efforts of the Gowāllās to organize and to promote behavior which would gain them a higher place in the social hierarchy of India :

1. The writer prefers the designation *upcasting* to Srinivas' *Sanskritization*, because each section of India has its own standards of high caste behavior, and often non-Sanskritic elements are part of these standards. Furthermore, just as Sanskritization is a form of upcasting, upcasting itself is a part of emulation (Lynch, 1968:235-238), which may be the cement which binds together a stratified society (Veblen, 1931:103-104).

> But the most important and effective sabha [conference] in the province is probably the Gope Jatiya Maha Sabha of the Goalas, or as they prefer to call themselves Ahirs, founded in 1912 and including members from the whole of the north of India from the Punjab to Bengal. The movement ... is described as a "Pan-Ahir movement"; sessions are held once a year and are attended by several thousands of persons. The association also has a monthly journal of its own ... "nothing less than Kshatriya position will satisfy it [the community]". ... A number of Ahirs have assumed the sacred thread [Tallents, 1023:236].

When the Gowāllās adopted the wearing of the sacred thread as a step in the process of upcasting, higher castes reacted violently to what they considered a disruption of the social order, as attested in the following :

> This action on their part was originally resisted ... by the higher castes such as the Rajputs and the Bhumihar Brahmans and led in some cases to violence and the criminal courts [ibid.].
>
> Inside the Hindu community, the efforts of the lower castes to improve their status led to considerable friction. ... The only movement which had any organization, however, was that of the Goalas, whose agitation extended to almost every district. ... A congress of Goalas known as the "Gop Jateya Sabha" was held in April, where different schemes for the advancement of the caste were projected [Anon., 1924:7].

The first All India Yadava Mahasabha (conference) was held in Allahabad in 1924; Yādāvā was adopted as a single name for all related cow-herding castes, replacing Ahir (Khedkar, 1959:v).

> The best instance of such a tendency to consolidate a number of castes into one group is to be found in the grazier castes which aim at combining under the term "Yādāvā" Ahirs, Goalas, Gopis, Idaiyans and perhaps some other castes of milkmen, a movement already effective in 1921 [Hutton, 1933:43].

And we know that the Gowāllās set their sights still higher as time went by from a statement of O'Malley :

> One caste, the Goalas of Bihar, were so little consistent that one year they claimed to be Vaisyas and another they wanted to climb higher and rank as Kshatriyas [O'Malley, 1932:171].

In reality, the Gowāllās were not inconsistent; they were constantly striving to move ever higher in caste rank. Today the Gowāllās claim they are Kshatriya, descended from Lord Krishna who was adopted by them. Evidence shows that even in 1921 the Gowāllās' claim to higher status was beginning to be accepted :

> The interest shown by the higher castes in resisting the caste claims of the Ahirs has weakened and it is probably owing to this fact that the operations of the Arya Samaj in North Bihar have not been so successful as they promised to be a few years ago [Tallents, 1923:237].

The Arya Samaj was the other string to the Gowāllās' bow. At one time local meetings of the Arya Samaj were held in the homes of prominent Gowāllās. A few people in the village still attend the annual Arya Samaj conference held in Patna. Today ritual behavior and caste position are dead issues among the various castes; discrimination in job and educational opportunities and conflicts in the political arena are the live issues.

Caste behavior, caste names, and family names (titles) also indicate what was happening to the Roy family. We can follow the changes in caste names through the present day Roy family (formerly Bhagat), but not in a straight line of progression, for upcasting is not a thread but a tapestry of the many separate efforts — local, regional, and national — to gain recognition. Overlap arises from confusion, from inconstancy in the individual's use of his caste's name, and from variations in social acceptance. Before 1930 all family documents recorded the caste name as Gowāllā; in that year, however, one document records the name as Ahir. In 1940, on a deed of sale, the Roys are for the first time designated as belonging to the Yādāvā caste. In

1941 a sale deed records both buyer and seller as Gowāllā-Yādāvā, showing the changeover of caste names. After 1942 the designation Yādāvā, with few exceptions, becomes standard.

By 1930 the name of the dairy had become Yādāvā Dairy Farms, as evidenced by its printed stationery (in English) and its postal receipts. The haste of the Roy family to adopt the name Yādāvā demonstrates their urgent desire to rise in the world by any and all means. The name Yādāvā was attached to the dairy in 1930 but not until 1942 does the name begin to appear regularly on sale deeds. It took twelve years for the community to accept fully the new class status of the Roys, so habitual had the use of the old name Gowāllā become. The evidence, as shown by the amount of land in their possession, indicates also another reason for the lag : the Roys, as contrasted with "some Goālās around Dinapore, who had made small fortunes in the butter trade" as early as 1907 (O'Malley, 1907:65), were premature in elaiming a higher social status for themselves. Incidentally, the designation of their shop in Calcutta as Lord Krishna's Dairy (the "patron saint" of the Yādāvās) was made for tax reasons.

Bahoren was the one in the family who took the initiative in using Roy as family name and Yādāvā as caste name. Calcutta had a large Yādāvā community; there the family learned that Nand Lall Roy was related to Lord Krishna, the "patron saint" of the Yādāvā. Calcutta was a familiar place to all the Roys; Dhaneshwer went to college there, Ram Chendra started to alternate there with Bahoren in 1926, and the others went there from time to time. The name Roy was first used in 1927, but not until the middle 1940's did it become firmly established. The older men tended to retain the name Bhagat; the younger preferred that of Roy. Other names adopted in the transition from Bhagat to Roy were Prasad, Yādāvā (as a family name), and Singh. This last name was suggested by one of the Yādāvā caste conferences in the mid 1930's and the people of Phulia Tola adopted it. But ever since the Roys came to live in the village, the name Roy has gradually replaced Singh, as the land sale deeds clearly show. Ram Chendra Roy put it bluntly : "We are leaders; they copied my title and my standard of living."* Among the Yādāvā up-casting has accompanied the building up

* Translated from Hindi.

of ranking within the caste, for all people do not economically better themselves to the same degree, nor do all people uniformly adopt the new standards of behavior. Those who have done well are more anxious, most sensitive, and had more to gain by adherence to the new standards than do those who have not done so well financially; for it is the *nouveaux riches* who strive to validate their status by up-casting. In the village, of course, the family most orthodox, best educated, and most strict about purdah is the Roy family.

Religion, as well as education and purdah, takes money. The village *purohit* (priest) apropos Hartula Kuar, remarked : "Only rich people can afford to be religious."* The more money you have the greater the number of religious ceremonies you can have and the more elaborate they may be. You can afford to pay a priest and make offerings; or make a pilgrimage to some distant shrine or holy place. The writer witnessed one ceremony where as part of the ritual a fire of sandalwood is kept burning. Ram Chendra Roy sat there throwing this expensive wood on the fire until it became almost as big as a bonfire. Only a rich man could afford to do that.

It is the successful people who form the elite, who supply the money, energy, brains, organization, and scholarship which it takes to pull a caste up. Families such as the Roys are prime examples. "Economic betterment thus seems to lead to the Sanskritization of the customs and way of life of a group (ibid., : 56)." Preceding the national Yādāvā caste conference, held in Patna in 1965, it was Parmeshwer Roy, head of the Roy family and *Mukhiya* (headman) of the village who scurried about raising approximately R. 5000 to help defray the cost of the conference. Already in 1907 O'Malley pointed out that wealthy members were the principal promoters of *pukka* caste behavior among the Gowāllās, just as the Roys are today. He refers to "some Goalas [*sic*] round Dinapore, who had made small fortunes in the butter trade, being among the most active supporters of the movement (1907:65)." The movement was an association for the protection of cattle, Gorakshini Sabhās. The likelihood was that it was this same affluent group who would cause O'Malley to complain twenty-five years later that the Gowāllās

* Translated from Hindi.

could not decide which of the two ranks to accept — Vaisyas or Kshatriyas.

By its very nature caste conferences, national and regional, provide the bases for interaction among the elite. It is this interaction, and specifically inter sub-caste marriage, which is starting to break down distinctions between the endogamous sub-castes and will lead to new internal rankings of the enlarged Yādāvā caste grouping. The elimination of sub-castes by inter-marriage and the use of one name for all the sub-castes is a stated goal of the Yādāvā.

Summary and Conclusions

The marriage of Hartola Kuar, a sister of five brothers, to Phagu Bhagat led to the gradual transfer of some of the members of her family to her home and to the participation of those family members in her husband's butter business. By living and working in Khagaul, the location of the butter shop, the newcomers learned the ways of the market.

Herding, milking, and trading in dairy products, the traditional occupations of their Gowāllā caste, gave the butter merchants of the Patna area an acquaintance with the business on a small scale. When the sale of dairy products was extended from local to distant markets and the volume of sales increased appreciably, butter merchants such as Phagu Bhagat and his rich brother, Lachman Bhagat, gave up herding and milking altogether and became middlemen, collecting their supplies of milk from others who remained herdsmen.

Poverty usually hastens the inevitable separation of the Indian joint family (Mandelbaum, 1968:32). In the case of the Roys, their separation and the formation of two additional branches of the family at Khagaul and Dinapore stemmed from their search for wealth.

With the increased productivity of their dairy, the Gowāllās in the Patna area were able to utilize ties with members of their own caste to furnish additional sources of supply as well as to aid them in establishing new markets for their products.

Because of their prosperity, the rich butter merchants were able to lead in upcasting both, themselves and other members of the caste. The prosperity of the Roy family also enabled them to buy land in villages near the market towns where their business was located. Siphai Bhagat's family eventually stopped buying land, quit the butter business, bought income-producing properties in the city and opened a new business. The Roys continued to buy land in Phulia Tola and eventually made their home there. Despite frictions which developed between them and the villagers, the Roys, after a struggle, succeeded in gaining control of the village.

To clarify the evolution of the fortunes of the Roy family and to put their relation to the village and market in clear perspective, the analysis will proceed diachronically through two main periods — the Khagaul and Phulia Tola periods. For it was when the Roys moved to Phulia Tola that a qualitative change in their social, economic, and political relationships came about.

Moore says : "Almost by definition economic innovations or those willing to become involved in new economic processes are marginal to the traditional order (1965:42)." If this means that people who are not doing well will have the motivation to do better, I agree. Such was the case with the Gowāllā caste living in the diara lands. Poverty was the push, and the possibility of something better, as exemplified in the case of Lachman (himself a Gowāllā), was the pull of the market. Later on Moore says : "The movement to the cities is partly ... a quest for economic opportunities better than those in rural areas (ibid : 72)." Thus the significance of Dhaneshwer Prasad's statement explaining why Lachman went into the butter business : "Anyone look after anything profitable"* is clearly one of economic motivation. This explains the movements from place to place; once the Roys had gotten a taste of a better life, their appetites were whetted for wealth and prestige. The problem was for the family to get from the village of Nilkanth Tola to the city. A relative living in town was the answer, for usually an Indian will not go to a strange place without an assurance of a house and food. The five brothers of the Roy family in Nilkanth Tola all had matrikin and affinals but only two lines were activated and both were in or near town. One, that of Hartola Kuar, a sister, was established at Khagaul; the other, that of Nanku's wife's father's household, was established on the outskirts of Dinapore. Thus a traditional pattern was followed in bringing them to the market place, and,

* Said in English.

once there, to train them in new ways. The socialization of the individual included the teaching of certain business skills.

The new ways, however, are in part the old ways, for the traditional occupation of the Gowāllās is herding, milking, making butter and *ghee*, and exchanging dairy products for other commodities; hence milk and butter-making are familiar occupations. When the market became important, the entrepreneur gave up milking himself. The increased demand stimulated an increase in production. The increase in demand and production raised their economic functions to a new level.

While the markets had always been there, the British gave a new stimulus to them, especially when the rail-road connection made Calcutta, for all practical purposes, a local market. The invention of the cream separator allowed sufficient production by a family-centered enterprise to supply the increased demand. New elements — the rail-road, the cream separator, the expanded market — joined with old elements of caste and family occupation. In Hoselitz' words : "Traditionally transmitted norms are not accepted because they exist, but because they fill a need to have rules in a given situation [1961:98]."

Dhaneshwer Prasad once explained to the writer how the joint family functions :

> In joint family there are many works we have to do; every member takes every department, as my Parmeshwer Babu looks after the business at Khagaul; I took after the business at Calcutta; Ram Chendra is looking after the cultivation. If we have not joint, there will be one person have to manage the three — it impossible. It is why we have departmental things.*

Here, it is evident, an old institution was converted to fit the need for a new division of labor.

Most important was the family's being situated in the market itself. Aside from the obvious direct business advantages, the location in a market meant the Roy family were positioned in the hub of communications networks (Bohannan and Dalton, 1965:19). Full-time participation in the market added extra

---

* Said in English.

economic and social increments to their life. While they sat and chatted on the well-worn benches in the verandah of the dairy, they were acquiring knowledge; they were the hub of a communications network, a center of information. Their conversation was not idle gossip for they were getting information to the end that they might know more than any one person talking to them.

This practice continues. Parmeshwer (the current head of the Roy family) takes up his post by the cash box under the verandah in full view of the street, seven days a week, from morning until night. Having a permanent place of business also meant that anybody who wanted to find them could do so easily. Accessibility and centrality allowed them to deal in cows, money, and land successfully; to find out about law and courts, and to assume the proper social behavior. This last they learned especially in Calcutta. The opportunities opened up by the market were not passed over by the Roys.

Among the results of the Roy's entrepreneurship were increase of wealth and elevation of social position. Since a family's social standing is in part determined by society's view of the family's caste, the Roys, just as other wealthy caste men in the past, were motivated to make efforts on behalf of their village (composed almost entirely of Yādāvās) and their caste. Another important result was the extension of their land holdings. By putting their profits in land the Roys were adhering to traditional Indian values. Kram Nresh, a member of the Roy's extended family, said : "It is a custom in India to buy land for the children, and it is considered wealth. Instead of putting the money in the dairy or a business, we buy land with savings."* This was done also by Siphai Bhagat and his family in Dinapore. Siphai, however, stopped after accumulating two hundred acres.

In order to oversee the land which they had acquired in the village of Phulia Tola the family eventually moved there. It was in the new house that the joint family, founded by Bhikhari and Bahoren, finally came together under one roof. Hartola Kuar spent the last six months of her life in the new house. Poverty had separated the joint family at Nilkanth Tola; wealth made possible the establishment of two new joint families, the

* Translated from Hindi.

Roys and Siphai Bhagat and his brothers, who with their families live jointly today at Nya Tola.

The move from Khagaul at first brought the Roy family into conflict with the village but ultimately the village fell under their control. New as well as old factors contributed to this control. Beidelman considers "numerical or political superiority and land tenure as the two most important determinants of economic power [1959:31]." (Although he was talking about caste and jajmani relationships, it is also true for a family vis-à-vis a village). In the case of the Roys political power was achieved through land tenure and maintained and extended by police force and court action. At the moment of the fight in the cane fields, the Roys were making up for their lack of numbers by invoking an extra-village component, the police. They pursued their enemies through the courts. Market people were calling upon market instrumentalities for help. Since then, by bringing in relatives and making alliances with certain village families, they also prepared themselves to play the village game by having numbers on their side.

Their wealth and its resultant prestige gave them influence in the newly constituted Panchayat, allowed them to form their own Cooperative Society, and secured for one of their men an administrative post concerned with village irrigation. Obviously the Roy family has consolidated its position in the village.

The story of the Roy family demonstrates the specific part played by the traditional social structure in the changing economic conditions which obtained in the Dinapore-Khagaul area in the early part of this century. The family was looking for a way out of poverty and the social structure provided a way out through the market.

However, their success in the market did not make them entrepreneurs in the classical Western sense, which is both to take risks and to manage. Their risk-taking was minimal, confined to giving advance money for cows. The sale of butter required neither salesmen nor inventory. It was their managerial function, however, which may stamp them as entrepreneurs as defined by Belshaw, which is "to take advantage of opportunities with an orientation towards expansion [1965:116]" and to form backward and forward links from source of supply to customer (ibid.:122). Their activity satisfied Belshaw's second criterion.

Siphai shows initiative and comprehension when he goes to Aligarh twice to get the separator and finally comes back with it and a distributorship as well. In time, the Roys too get the machine; both demonstrate managerial skill in organizing and reorganizing continually the collection of milk. Bahoren discovers a way to bind his suppliers to him with advance money and to get milk cheaper.

It is clear, however, that, to the extent that they do not "take advantage of opportunities with an orientation towards expansion" (in Belshaw's terms), the Roys are not in the full sense entrepreneurs (loc. cit.). Unlike Western businessmen who will always invest a sizable share of their profits in improving plant equipment, the Roy family have invested — through advance money — mainly to strengthen their supply of milk[1] but have neglected new methods of butter production. Consequently the business has difficulty today in meeting competition from manufacturers with modern equipment. After the cream separator and the metal churn, the only improvement in the last few years was the addition of a cold storage room necessary to maintain butter at the minimum butter-fat content prescribed by the Calcutta authorities. Apart from that, no money has been invested in the business since the day of its founding. For this reason, therefore, the Roys are entrepreneurs only minimally.

Quite in contrast to their indifferent concern with the growth of their butter business, the Roys display great interest in the acquisition and improvement of the land and its crops. They were the first to get better seeds and fertilizer, the first to grow potatoes in the village as a cash crop. They constantly replace their older oxen with younger ones, and the oxen get the best of veterinary care. In 1957 they installed a tube-well operated by diesel power to provide water for irrigation. When this brought insufficient water and proved expensive, they abandoned it in favor of a new electric tube-well. To obtain electricity took persistence because of the red tape involved with the government which controls electricity in that area. They succeeded, and now fields which formerly could be cultivated only in certain seasons are fertile the year round. Furthermore, they initiated action to get additional outlets dug from the irrigation canal. (Early

1. I am grateful to Dr. Joan Mencher for bringing this to my attention.

in the writer's stay they pressed him into action to compose and type letters to the government requesting the new outlets.) By purchasing land adjacent to present land, they consolidated plots. Whenever the government wanted a plot to demonstrate a new method of agriculture or a new seed, the Roys volunteered one of their own.

One of the Roys articulated quite clearly, even though in broken English, the views of the family concerning the importance of land as contrasted with business :

> How will he get his rice and food, if he has not cultivate ? We purchase land to get food. ... Your country is the business man and here is more cultivators, eighty per cent are cultivators here. ... We keep money enough for the dairy, to start dairy and extra money goes to the land. ... The money always does not remain in hand, and that money is in land, that will be the property; and the cash money, we like land more than business. If sometimes poverty comes, cash money is out of stock. We are cultivators; we like to cultivate more land, and when poverty comes, what men will do ? Cash money is empty, there is no business, how will we live ? That land is the saving. Money is first of all cash money; afterwards ornaments and the land. ... The extra money is always engaged in land. That is the sign of extra money, an extra from the business. We keep only business enough money, and extra money is given to landed properties. ... We have not so interest in dairy than land. We are Indian people. More like landed. ... This land is also business. It also makes money.*

(Similar thoughts had been voiced by Hira Lall and Ram Nresh previously). Such thoughts are foreign to Western concepts of business enterprise, where the business itself is valued.

The concept of business as the road to a secure future is also foreign to the Roys. Their business merely provides the means for the realization of traditional values in a traditional setting. Their success in business was translated into success within the

---

* Said in English.

social structure and served to reinforce its traditions. Basically their attitude towards land remained that of the peasant.

This attitude is also revealed in the custom, long established among the Roys, of designating a member of the family as an overseer of their lands. He is always the oldest male member of the family, one who has retired from active participation in the family business but is still capable of overseeing the hired supervisor and his laborers. He functions, in short, as a family watchdog. Consequently, little prestige attaches to the job.

From their attitude towards land we might conclude that the Roys are traditional Indians. Not at all. There remains, however, a certain orientation towards the market. In thought and deed the Roys face away from the village, for their heart and work are in town. Except for the old man who oversees the lands, they are commuters. When the farm work is done, even the old overseer changes into his good clothes and walks to the dairy in Khagaul.

The separateness of the Roy family from the other villagers was brought into focus one day when Parmeshwer Roy, head of the family and Mukhiya (headman) of the Panchayat, dismissed a question at a Panchayat meeting by saying, "I am a businessman."* There is a minimum of interaction between them and the village.

The anomalous position of the Roys as residents and landowners of Phulia Tola who want only town occupations is exemplified by the choice of the man of the family who takes care of their most important possession — the land. He is always an old man in semi-retirement. The job carries no prestige, for though land is the traditional value, business and government attract the young and the educated. As Ram Chendra Roy put it, "they want to sit in an office under a fan, while here they have to be in the sun and talk to ignorant people."** The paradox is that now it is he who supervises the agriculture and walks to the dairy at the end of the day, although most of his life was spent in selling butter in Calcutta. Arensburg explains this shift : "Social arrangements make their own values in the process of becoming culture patterns, or 'instituted.' ... Action comes first ...

---

* Translated from Hindi; but "businessman" was said in English.

** Translated from Hindi.

values come second [1957:104, 195]." Association with the market has given them a preferred status, even though originally the market was regarded merely as the means towards the ownership of land. Arensberg's explanation suggests that repeated participation in the market has become a value in itself.

This change in values explains why the Roys endeavored to gain ascendancy over a village in which they had no interest. For once they bought land in Phulia Tola, they had no choice but to stay there to protect their investment by every means. They moved into the village to guard their land, and they made sure they stayed in the village for the same reason. At the time of their crisis, the Roys relied primarily upon the political apparatus of the market for aid. Because money was invested in land, land had to be watched, and to accomplish this the Roys were forced into the social, economic, and political structure of the village. Even though their money was made in the larger sphere of town, they had to participate in the smaller village sphere. While the Roys lived in Khagaul, their economy and the village economy were differently emplaced; but their move to the village and their eventual control of the village was a tacit recognition that their true interests lay not in the market but in the village and its culture.[1]

A contrast must be drawn and a change noted. Unlike the Roy family of Khagaul and Phulia Tola, the Siphai Bhagat branch stopped buying land at a certain point and because of circumstances went out of the dairy business and into an entirely new venture — the cold storage business. Since they reinvested part of their profits in business rather than all of it in land, they became entrepreneurs under the classical conditions of risk and management. More importantly, the enterprise reveals a change of values. The writer does not know definitely how this came about, but because the younger members of Siphai's family are in charge (unlike the Roys where the older men are still in charge), he suspects they are the ones who instituted the change. Incidentally, that family still maintains the dairy, though it functions now only as a meeting place. Hira Lall told him that if they tore it down the family's prestige would suffer. This illustrates, again, a market orientation.

---

1. I am indebted to Prof. C. M. Arensberg for bringing to my attention this change in embeddiment.

Among the Roys' family there was once an abortive revolt. The dairy had been losing business in Calcutta to more progressive competitors. Some of the younger men (with the help of one of the older men) wanted to improve the operation of the dairy; they even bought some equipment, but the other two, older men, obstructed their efforts and the attempt failed. However, the family takes every opportunity to buy land. Once they had to borrow money from the writer to tide them over while they were buying land. For the older generation investment in land, rather than business, continues to have highest priority. In this respect they behave like the rest of the village.

After his efforts to improve the dairy were thwarted, the son tried a business of his own in another field. When it failed, he got a job in the Bihar State Electricity Board through the influence of his uncle, Ram Gopal, who has a high position in the state government. Another member of the family, the youngest of the five brothers, is a construction contractor. Two of the young men work in the dairy. Those who are in school and who are almost ready to assume adult roles expect to go into government service or a profession. These men make evident the new paths of mobility in urban life with its attendant values.

If we look at the younger generation of the two families, we can see a change in them away from their parents. The difference between the two generations lies in the fact that the older was only partially committed to market values, while the younger generation, having known nothing else, is fully committed. Unlike his once poor father, the rich man's son has no land hunger. After all, he was born owning land.

CHAPTER IV

PHULIA TOLA : THE ECONOMIC DEVELOPMENT OF A VILLAGE

According to the stories of the old men, Phulia Tola was founded in 1857 by Phulia Devi who came from the vicinity of Jagdishpur in Shahabad District, approximately twenty-five miles west of the village. The Indian patriot Kuar Singh, who led the uprising against the British had his headquarters there.

Phulia means "flower" and *Devi* is equivalent to English "Mrs." We know she was widowed at a young age; otherwise the village would have been named after her husband. For it is a common practice to name even local sites after their founders. The writer was once shown a house, somewhat apart from the main cluster of houses, in which lived an old man, Sadhu, with his married children and grandchildren. Since he was the one who built the house, people smilingly referred to that north-western corner of the village as "Sadhu Tola." (*Tola* means "small village" with no implication of being part of a larger place.) If more houses are built near Sadhu, someday Sadhu Tola may become a village of its own.

The date given by the villagers for the founding of Phulia Tola is 1857, the year of the Sepoy Mutiny. In that year, Phulia Devi is said to have fled from Arrah (Shahabad District) about twenty-five miles to the west to escape the fighting, but no one really knows. Famine, flood or oppressive taxation might equally have been the causes. The genealogy of the family, however, tends to support the date. Since Phulia Devi and others had to move their houses to make room for the irrigation canal forming the eastern boundary of Phulia Tola which the British completed in 1877 (O'Malley, 1907:109), the date of 1857 seems reasonable. Inasmuch as the events in Phulia Tola will be related to historical trends, the date of the founding of the village has importance.

Phulia Devi and her husband built their mud hut with its straw-thatched roof a few hundred yards from the dirt road which leads to the town of Khagaul, and a little over a mile north of the village of Bhasola Danapore. In both places lived people of her own caste and sub-caste. Three miles to the east was Phulwari Sharif and eight miles through the fields lay the capital of Bihar, Patna. And everywhere between were villages and hamlets. For an Indian villager, these are all within walking distance. One man in the village, a notorious cheapskate, is noted for walking eight miles to Patna and eight miles back every day to save carfare. Bodies are carried ten miles to a certain burning ghat on the bank of the Ganges where the inhabitants of Phulia Tola traditionally have burned their dead. (The writer once set out to witness such a ceremony and people assured him that it was quite all right to ride to the scene — as twelve of his fellow villagers climbed aboard his small Landrover.)

When Phulia Devi's husband died, her sons were probably old enough to work the fields, otherwise, she would have returned to her husband's village. It is fair to surmise that she cultivated some land and kept cattle. At that time all of Phulia Tola was scrub land and forest, but a plentiful supply of water made the area attractive to cattle raisers. Before the canal was built a tributary of the Son River flowed through the village; then the tributary was diverted to provide more water for the canal. As one might expect, the water table is only twelve feet beneath the surface of the soil. This meant that even if the monsoon failed, the farmers could irrigate the rice crop by water drawn from dirt wells. These would last for a few seasons before caving in. It also meant that during the rest of the year other crops could be grown which did not need the abundant supply of water necessary for rice cultivation. Wells and tanks (small reservoirs) were frequently used for irrigation before the British extended the irrigation canals. Even after the canals were dug, Phulia Tola was irrigated by dirt wells in those places where the canal water did not reach. During the drought of the last few years, dirt wells have been revived and stood the inhabitants of the village in good stead. In part, Mukerjee had this to say about the agricultural situation in this region between 1600 and 1800 :

> On the whole, however, more valuable crops were grown and both revenue and productivity were greater in Bihar than in the U.P. ... A bigha near Jaunpur, Benares or Patna yielded on an average as much as two bighas

> between Agra and Saharanpur at the time of Akbar, according to Moreland's estimate [194?:8].

Mukerjee also specifically mentioned Patna and Shahabad as extending their acreage in the nineteenth century (ibid.). Phulia Devi and those who came after her were thus part of a movement in history.

Phulia Devi undoubtedly had as many cattle as she and her two sons and two daughters could take care of, for grazing lands stretched for miles. For some of this land she had to pay rent to the zamindar;[1] but to get rice-growing plots she had also to pay for land for which she had no use. An ex-zamindar of Phulia Tola explained the system :

> At that time all the land was not fertile; some was high land, some was low land; now the land has been made fertile. Land was not all fertile at that time. Some places it was high land, some places it was low land. People have made it fertile. ... If you come first it doesn't mean I should give you all the food; and when the others come, I won't be able to feed them.*

The zamindar wanted his land to yield rent, either in the form of crops or cash. But not all land was fertile or suited to the cultivation of all crops. In every negotiation for land it, therefore, became necessary that a compromise be effected. To get rice land the *ryot* (cultivator) would have to take both high land and barren land. High land was suitable for growing crops such as fodder, corn, wheat, and potatoes, which did not need the amount of water required for rice. The result was that any one ryot would have lands in different fields. If he sold land, he would do the same thing : make the new owner take some of the bad land with the good. This system of parcelling plots according to their fertility is clearly shown in the earliest land records (1910) where each plot is designated as rice, high, or barren land.

---

1. Neale has shown that neither "rent" nor "tax" is the proper term (1957:218-236), but for convenience I will follow the British usage and call it rent.

*Translated from Hindi.

This practice continues today; when a man buys land he must take at least two types, which means his plots are scattered at a distance from each other.

The breakup of a joint family also contributes to the scattering of plots, as well as to their diminution. When a joint family separates, rather than assign whole plots as each person's share, the family will divide each plot into equal shares. The reason for dividing land in this way is that no two plots are equal, either in size or yield. The peasant's concern about the fairness of the division of plots in relation to yield was strikingly demonstrated to the writer when he tried to discuss the hypothetical case of two plots located in different parts of the village but exactly alike in all other respects. Then would each family member take one plot as his share ? The informant attacked the hypothesis itself : "No, we could not be sure," he said, "that the plots were exactly alike." He also implied that, rather than risk disputes — and these could be acrimonious — over the allocation of plots, they would prefer the division of each separate plot, even though the *ārís* (low earthen walls) erected to mark the boundaries might reduce the acreage of the newly formed plots considerably. He even knew precisely how many pounds of rice would be lost as a consequence. (Incidentally, this knowledge indicates that land is so scarce, and hence valuable, that it is measured in terms of pounds of rice.)

Through the years, the result of sharing land in this way has been, obviously, to decrease the size of the plots. In addition, the separation of the joint family allows the individual member now to sell his share. Consequently, to buy the same amount of land, the purchaser today must accept smaller and more widely scattered plots than he would have in the past. Thus the original system of allocation of land and the separation of joint families both account for the crazy-quilt pattern of land ownership found in any Indian village.

Furthermore, the original system of land allocation in part accounts for members of the same extended family living contiguous to each other. Traditionally zamindars gave house land rent free. As families expanded they built next to each other. When the rent was permanently settled in this area in 1911-12, the houses existing then had their tax exemption continued. Now, if a house is built on what used to be agricultural land, the owner must pay rent; so the tendency has been to subdivide the old houses. This leads to the characteristic pattern of Indian villages in Bihar — a cluster of houses in one place, a few scattered houses on the outskirts.

With the exception of three families, Phulia Tola is a one-caste village and is, therefore, dependent to an unusual extent on other places, notably the town of Khagaul and, to a lesser degree, the next door village of Bhasola Danapur to supply necessary services. The *pāndit* (priest), the *burEhī** (carpenter), the *hạlwẹ̄* (sweet-maker and cook), and the *dhobị* (washerman) who serves only the Roys come from Khagaul. The *hājạm* (barber and religious functionary), and his wife, the *hājạmīn*, and the *dhobī* who serves the rest of the village come from Bhasola Danapur. About ten years ago the Roy family invited a *lohạr* (blacksmith) family into the village; until then the villagers had relied on a blacksmith in Khagaul and others elsewhere. Many people still prefer to go to those blacksmiths. The *khūmhạr* (potter), the *mālī* (florist), the *bhathī* (brickmaker), the *pāndit* who officiates at funerals — all come from places outside the village. The regular *pạndit*, the *hājām* and *hājạmīn*, and the *burEhē* are in a jajmani relationship with the people of the village. The only families in the village who do not belong to the Yādāvā caste are the aforementioned Lohārs and another family, *kānū*, whose traditional occupation is frying flat rice and repairing roofs. It is logical to assume, as do the villagers, that the surrounding towns and villages have always supplied Phulia Tola with their services.

On all counts, Phulia Tola, in the past as today, was an excellent location for a new arrival. A market for selling milk products and for buying anything needed was nearby. The town on the north and the village on the south supplied the lobor and the various skills, physical and ritual, which an Indian demanded. Once it had been cleared, the land yielded a comfortable livelihood. With grazing lands all around, cows supplied ample milk for consumption and for ready sale in town.

Phulia Devi's decision to settle in Phulia Tola was, therefore, a logical one and equally logical was the settlement that followed

---

*I have added the following to Klass's system of notation of sounds (1961:xxiv-xxv) E the "e" of English "bet" (L.S.).

in her wake. The key to the existence of Phulia Tola is voiced in the village expression, "to eat and to earn." To eat is to grow your own food; to earn is to have some way of getting money, whether by the sale of a commodity, or by service, or by entrepreneurship.

Phulia Devi had two sons, Naubat and Daulat, and one daughter, Teteri. All married, and, as was usual, Teteri went to live with her husband, Jai Ram, at his village in the west diara. She did not like to eat corn, meaning that the soil was not fertile, and so returned to Phulia Tola with her husband. After her death her husband remarried and brought his new wife, Totia, into the village. In time, Totia called her brother Bhabichan to live with her, for Bhabichan was poor. In due course, Totia's husband, Jai Ram, arranged the marriage of his brother-in-law, Bhabichan. Phulia Devi's sons, Naubat and Daulat, both married and remarried when their wives died; between them they fathered eleven sons and four daughters, who in turn married. Through subsequent interconnections via daughters, they are by far the largest family in the village. Those in the direct line of descent from Phulia Devi are called collectively the Mahātō (headman) family, because until the inauguration of the official panchayat system in Bihar in 1947, it was this family which supplied the headman of the village. We have already seen how the greater participation in the market by the Roy family allowed them to successfully challenge the authority and prestige of the Mahātō group.

Phulia Devi had a sister, Lauthi, who married Ram Kewal; eventually they moved to Phulia Tola. They produced a son, Sheo Lall, and a daughter, Samjharia, who married and left the village. Sheo Lall had three sons and a daughter. They are the next largest family in the village.

The above material on the beginnings of the first two families into the village is a selection from different versions. Where kinship accounts differed, the version given by the person most closely related was given preference; a knowledge, also, of the traditions of the village allowed for logical choices to be made. According to one version, for example, Ram Kewal was Phulia Devi's brother; the writer prefers to believe they were brother and sister-in-law, for if they had been brother and sister, the village would have been named after him, instead of

Phulia Devi, and the families might not have been on different sides when the village eventually split into factions. One account, also, had Totia as a sister of Teteri, instead of the second wife of Teteri's husband. The writer doubts this version, for, if it were true, Bhabichan would have been the brother of Teteri also and, of course, would have been born in the village. This did not square with the facts. However, all were agreed that the above were all related, just as they were agreed that one of the men who married a woman in Phulia Devi's family came from Panapur, which is one mile north of the Cantonment. It may have been Jai Ram.

Whoever this man was, he was a *gaon bhai* (village brother) of Das Mar and Bharosa, who had married sisters and were, therefore, related as brothers. It is a plausible surmise that Das Mar and Bharosa knew about this new settlement, which was six or seven miles south of them, from the man or men who married Phulia Tola girls. Sometime after Das Mar and Bharosa moved in, Khakhanu, also from Panapur, came too. He was a close friend of Tilak, Das Mar's second son. The pattern of marriage and visiting, which has been previously described, allows for close inter-village friendships, especially if you are of the same caste and sub-caste, as are all the families in Phulia Tola except for five out of some seventy-four. Das Mar, Bharosa, and Khakhanu account for the arrival of the third, fourth, and fifth families in the village.

The history of the beginnings of the first two families — and their extensions — who came to Phulia Tola illustrates the role of fictive as well as true kinship in settling the village. It is the security of these two types of attachment which primarily induces the outsider to move. The only prior affiliation of the third category of families who immigrated to the village was membership in the same caste and sub-caste as the others. This in itself gave them an identity with the village and marked it as a congenial place to live. Along with Mayer, the writer would emphasize the sub-caste as the important operational unit of caste (1960:270-275). Furthermore, this last group of families had, as late arrivals, an advantage over the original settlers : the village was already well established.

The process by which men of this nonkinship-affiliated group came to live in Phulia Tola was explained to Ram Chendra Roy by Lall Bihari (whom the writer was questioning in his office in front of a tape recorder), using Dukhit as an example :

> Just as you are a rich man, and you keep others — just so he left his job and started living here. He has no relations here. You remember Siri. I brought him here, and it was because of me that he got a place to live in your house. He started working for you; he started working in your fields; I got your father to give him some money, and he started working. After living here for some time, he got cattle, married off his daughter. This is the way it happens to other people also.*

Lall Bihari then reminded Ram Chendra that the Roys, themselves, had brought two families related to them to Phulia Tola. Dukhit had had a job working with the rail-road in Khagaul. More than just recounting the story of Dukhit, Lall Behari was explaining how a newcomer gets his start; naturally, with relatives it was that much easier.

To show the significance of kinship for migration to the village, the following figures are presented. They include the above histories and the Roy family. The eleven men who came as strangers provide an important contrast to the twenty-seven men who had prior family affiliation.

When you eliminate the four men whose histories have been given (including the Roy family), only one of those families remaining has other than minor importance. Two of them came because of the Roy family — one a business acquaintance and the other a blacksmith family. Lall Bihari has already told about Siri. A family that fries rice and fixes roofs, and a man who had trouble in another village and had to leave — these complete the roster of non-affiliated families.

*Translated from Hindi.

FAMILY CONNECTIONS AT TIME OF SETTLEMENT

Not known family connection :		11
Men who came in via a wife		
Wife's affiliation was consanguineal :	18	
Wife's affiliation was affinal :	3	
Total		21
Men who came in without a wife's affiliation :		
(Consanguineally — mother, sister, daughter) :		6
Total		42

To return to the original point. Kinship has played an important role in populating the village. From male ego's point of view, the largest single group of migrants activated affinal lines, i.e., they moved uxorilocally. The second largest group who activated kinship ties moved gynoconsanguineally.* These two groups together compose the most significant group, those who moved gynolocally.*

Just as a man seeking to purchase an animal, or to borrow money, or to obtain an appraisal on land, or to arrange a marriage will consult first with his kinship circle, so too will he think of consulting them before deciding where to move. Since in Phulia Tola, in common with most north Indian villages, patrilineality and virilocality are the rule, the villager must resort to his female kin when he leaves his natal village. Thus, when a peasant in northern India moves his family, gynolocality (largely ignored in the literature — Mayer mentions it *en passant* (1960:273) becomes the important factor : virilocality determines the peasant's destination; gynolocality establishes the route he follows.

Land and the market attracted people to the village and kinship provided the route for getting there.

Except for the people brought in by the Roy family, immigration to the village has practically stopped because, as the evidence indicates, the land has reached the limit of its carrying capacity.

*Since anthropology is deficient in terms for describing these phenomena, the writer has undertaken to devise them.

In one instance a man turned away a distant relative because he could not afford to keep him. This same man hounds his mother's brother's widow, who lives in the village, for payment for her house land, which she claims was already made to her late brother-in-law but for which she did not receive a deed of sale. There are two other cases like this current in the village. Payment is now demanded to execute a deed of conveyance for land sold or given in the past to a relative. These are evidences of economic strain.

Since the village is supported mainly by agriculture, the scarcity and high price of land is the best evidence of this strain. The villagers who attribute the scarcity of land to the increase in population through the years are conscious of population as a problem. The writer knows of two men who had vasectomies, one of them was the same man, Ram Ratan, who turned away his distant relative and was trying to get money from his mother's brother's widow. Besides owning land, he keeps a pony cart for hire and works in Khagaul in a cloth shop. Evidently Ram Ratan finds it difficult to make ends meet.

When Sukhari "Mistri," the other man who had the operation, told the writer about it, his father protested that one should have all the children that God gave; Sukhari dismissed his father's objection by saying seven children were enough.

The following table is the first step in establishing a man-land ratio in order to see what possible effect population has had on the village. The 1950 and 1957 figures were gathered by the secretary of the panchayat; the writer did those for 1965. The 1910 figures are extrapolated from the land records which were prepared in that year. Each household, along with the adult males who had shares in that land, was listed separately. Since the writer has no way of knowing the number of children and females, the 1910 figures arc given as an index. The 1920 figure is an estimate made by two of the old men prior to the writer's arrival in the village. They had been discussing the rise in population but, interestingly enough, counted only men and boys. It should be noted that the following table includes both increases resulting from immigration and natural increase.

POPULATION OF PHULIA TOLA

	1910	1920	1950	1957	1965
Men	51		102	133	169
Boys		80*	100	128	144
Women			113	132	156
Girls			75	111	101
Total			390	504	507
Homes	25		48	67	74

*Total of men and boys

The upward trend in the population of Phulia Tola was characteristic of India as a whole (Davis, 1951:85-90).

LAND INDEX OF PHULIA TOLA

	1910	1950	1957	1965
Amount of Land (in acres)	81.727	101.777	113.695	126.422
Acres per Adult Male	1.6	1.0	.86	.75

Since the Roys own more land than the rest of the village combined, the inclusion of their acreage would give a false picture; hence, their land and their family have been omitted.

Although the accuracy of the figures may be questioned, the man-land index does serve to indicate a decrease in the relative amount of land available to support the population through the years. The rather recent insufficiency of arable acreage is the single most important factor in the evolution of the village's economy.

The figures for the amount of land in 1910 are accurate, for in that year the British completed their cadastral survey, which mapped and numbered all plots, including tax-free house land, they conferred ownership on the man actually on the land; whether cultivating or herding; and they distributed documents (*khātīyāns*) which recorded the name and village of the owner (and the shares if more than one man in the family owned it), the numbers, boundaries, and type of land of each plot. Today *khātīyāns* have the force of original deeds of title.

The last time any official record was made of each family's holdings was in 1910; not even the tax collector has an up-to-date record. Even in the survey of 1910 mistakes were made which, never having been corrected, cause disputes to this very day. The writer was once asked to try and persuade a man to correct such an error by executing a deed of sale. Though the beneficiary freely acknowledged the long-standing error, he refused to correct it, undoubtedly wanting money for a good deed.

In view of the lack of records summarizing holdings, it is difficult to know the amount of land under village control in any one year. The procedure adopted was to obtain, record, and summarize all documents pertaining to land held by the villagers. (The head of the Roy family, by giving the writer his family's documents, set the example for the rest of the village. Everyone cooperated, with one exception. His records were copied from an official source.) The deficiencies of the record so obtained are many.

Since only the purchaser receives a document upon the sale of land, and since the writer had access only to the villagers' papers, it is possible that some village land was lost to outsiders without its coming to his knowledge. (The Roys are considered here as outsiders). The villagers, for whom land is the most important acquisition in their lives assured the writer, however, that no land was sold to non-villagers. The writer's own observations confirm the tenacity with which the peasant holds onto his land. Fair means and foul are used to keep the land within the family. It is important to recognize that alienation of land destroys the peasant's economic base. When one brother, a ne'er-do-well, threatened to sell his share of the land, his two older brothers beat him and ran him out of the village. In another case, the only one of its kind to the writer's knowledge, a villager had to buy back his own land from his married daughters in order to keep the family property intact. They had invoked their legal right to their share of it; this was unusual, for according to village custom the daughter's dowry is considered her share in the family property. The tendency to cultivate nearby land also would militate against land leaving the possession of the village. Moreover, the records of the Roys reveal that of their vast holdings in the vicinity of Phulia Tola only an insignificant percentage of land was bought from the inhabitants of the village.

Mortgaging, like the sale of land, requires documents; the mortgagee receives a deed noting the terms of the transaction; this is returned to the mortgagor when he pays off the mortgage. Until he does, the mortgagee cultivates the land. Usually the mortgagee is protected from repayment for three years. No one could state with certainty the maximum time limit; one man thought it might be for sixty years. Customarily a mortgage can run indefinitely. Occasionally a mortgage bears interest; then the mortgagor himself cultivates his land. Since it is usual for the mortgagee to cultivate the land, in order to have an accurate year-by-year account of the land under village control, mortgages should be included. It is comparatively easy to obtain reliable information from each family about current mortgages; the difficulty lies in recapturing the past. When a mortgage is part of the condition of the purchase of land, the deed is retained by the buyer; otherwise it is destroyed. Mortgages, like deeds of sale, are recorded, but, even if permission were granted, endless searching would be required to locate the records. For this reason mortgages are omitted from the land table.

As land has become scarce, mortgaging has acquired a new importance. Since the mortgagee cultivates the land, and since the amount of money he has given the mortgagor is customarily half the value of the land, financing a mortgage becomes a cheap way to secure land to cultivate. In all probability, coincident with the populating of the land there has been a shift away from the interest-bearing mortgage to the right-to-cultivate type. In the latter and more usual case, the mortgagee can work the land himself or rent it. Often, as part of the mortgage transaction, the owner of the land becomes the tenant.

Most sales of land today are conversions from mortgages, giving another dimension to the system. However, the land is not always sold to the mortgagee. This was especially true of the Roy family who, besides their own, systematically took over others' mortgages and when the mortgagor needed cash would force him to sell his property to them. The scarcity of land for sale is matched by the paucity of lending agencies; therefore, when a poor landholder needs money, rich men such as the Roys usually step in to satisfy the demand for cash but on terms favorable to themselves. This is probably the reason why people in Phulia Tola seldom sold or mortgaged their land to the Roy family but made every effort to retain them within their own extended families. Land mortgaged to the Roys made the mortgagor susceptible to their pressure; land sold to them was lost forever; and, in general, land conveyed to the already wealthy Roys increased their power.

Sometimes a landholder wants to expand his holding but lacks the cash necessary for the purchase of other properties, especially when the opportunity arises unexpectedly. These infrequent opportunities must be grasped quickly. In such cases he will approach the other landholder who is in need of funds, and offer the money in return for a mortgage on the man's property. If he succeeds, he will, in turn, mortgage his own property to provide the money for the first transaction. There are both risks and advantages in such transactions. What the first man hopes is that he will earn enough to redeem his own mortgage and that the second man will continue the original indebtedness to him or even increase it further, ultimately going so far into debt that the property will easily fall into his hands. Since the mortgagee has the right to plow the mortgagor's lands during the period of indebtedness, the mortgagee is perfectly willing to continue the arrangement indefinitely. The man who "gives", (that is to say, mortgages) his land hopes someday to get it back; he retains his grip on it. Ganga Bisun told the writer, with noticeable pride in his own cleverness, how, needing R. 3,000 for a wedding, instead of one mortgage at R. 3,000, he had mortgaged to the same man three parcels of land for R. 1,000 each. This would make it easier for him to repay his loan. Thus the two meet at a halfway house — the mortgagee on the road to full ownership, the mortgagor on the road to eventual loss. Each hopes for the best.

The third system of land tenure is tenancy. Basically there are two methods of renting land. In the first, *batē*, the tenant shares the crop equally with the landlord. Usually the crop is divided after it has been threshed. In the second type of tenancy a fixed amount of cash or crops is agreed on in advance as the fee for renting the land. Landowners like the fixed-fee basis for it eliminates risk. All agree it is better to plow your own land than to rent it to a tenant, for he does not take proper care of it. The Roys are by far the largest single source of land for rent, with approximately half of their ninety-three acres cultivated by tenants. Rather than the trouble of supervising their agricultural labor force, the Roys would prefer to put all their land in the hands of tenants; the fear, however, of the village then being about to control them dissuades them.

The lands lying on both sides of the canal and owned by the canal company are another dependable source of lands for rent. These lands are never sold, and the rents are low. Preference, reinforced by a few rupees, is given to past tenants. There were, however, no records available to the writer for either the canal lands or other village lands rented during the years preceding his stay in Phulia Tola. This was also the problem concerning mortgages in the past. Consequently, it is impossible to establish a precise man-land ratio for the village. The index the writer has arrived at is based on ownership as determined by the records and is used as a key to assessing changes in population density throughout the years.

The most important variable not taken into account here is the improvement in agricultural production during the years. This has been done by the extension of irrigation, the removal of sandy and clayey soil, and the use of fertilizer and improved seeds. Other improvements, such as the lowering and leveling of the soil, double cropping, and the introduction of new crops were the result of the first two processes.

Before the irrigation canal was built people depended primarily on the monsoon rains, augmented by a small reservoir with dirt walls, to provide water. During the rice season the monsoon rains are supplemented by irrigation, which is nevertheless important, for it makes up for any slack and can be regulated. Crops grown during the winter and hot season depend on irrigation and wells. The Roys have their own electrically driven tube well for a small portion of their land.

As part of his *Final Report*, issued in 1914, James attributes much of the stability of life to irrigation :

> The district [of Patna] has not suffered severely in any of the great famines of the nineteenth century. The

> embankments and irrigation works maintained by the zamindars, though they do not afford efficient protection, serve to modify considerably the effects of floods or drought, to which the district would otherwise be specially liable. The agricultural population as a whole does not depend upon any single crop, and the people readily help themselves by growing *rabi* (spring) crops on a large area if their rice crop fails [James, 1914:4].

We know people were quick to take to a dependable source of water. "The demand for water is steadily increasing and the greater part of the supply is used for the irrigation of rice [O'Malley, 1907:109]." Rice was the preferred food, and irrigation made its cultivation possible. This statement also foreshadowed the problem of an adequate water supply. In the same year, 1907, James came close to pinpointing Phulia Tola :

> The cultivators are ... fairly well-to-do as compared with the cultivators in other parts of Bihar. Their holdings are generally sufficient for their maintenance. ... The most prosperous cultivators are those in the neighborhood of Bankipore, Patna, and Dinapore. A large cultivating class live on the outskirts of these towns and make a comfortable living by raising garden produce ... which are exported in large quantities to Calcutta and other parts of Bengal [pp. 129-130].

This description does not fully apply to Phulia Tola where milk was the "cash crop", some of it in the form of butter going to Calcutta (as we have seen in the history of the Roy family) where the price was set.

Strictly speaking, Phulia Tola is a cluster of houses, for there are no boundaries demarcating the village lands. Land owned by people who live in the village is Phulia Tola land, and this is scattered in three revenue divisions called *thānās*. However, the sub-canal on the west and the main canal on the east, about a half mile apart, do form natural boundaries of the village. Possibly the thana lines were drawn up before the canal and sub-canal were built, for they are ignored as borders on the cadastral maps of 1910. These maps show the existence in 1910 of three outlets for the western sub-canal; however, until 1925, in order to keep more water for themselves, the people of the next village prevented any westward flow. In that year, an official, encouraged by a gift of money from Phulia Tola, unblocked these outlets, which benefited some landowners of Phulia Tola. This sub-canal is but a trickle compared to the main canal, which is big enough to have borne a weekly steamer service in days gone by (O'Malley, 1907:109). Barges, mostly carrying hay from the hinterlands to Patna, still use it. Locally at least, no new outlets have been added to the original three in the sub-canal.

In contrast to this, the main canal, which according to the map had three outlets in 1910, has been tapped six more times since then. Sometime after 1910 three new outlets were opened in the main canal on the east. The water ran in an easterly direction. These new outlets plus the already existing reservoir provided a plentiful supply of water in that section where much of the village land was located. Not until 1937 did the area between the canals receive irrigation water; this was on the south side. In 1952 another opening on the north was built which also flowed towards the center (assuming the land between the canals, which contains the habitation site of the village, as the center). Another outlet, strategically placed, followed in 1961.

The existing facilities have not satisfied the demand; the writer was pressed into service to type up a petition for another outlet (which had not been acted upon when he left, a year later). The usual way to get water is to have its flow from field to field. During the rice growing season, when demand for water is at its maximum, disputes over water are an everyday occurrence. During this season men stay up all night irrigating their fields, either because it is their turn to do so or because it is not their turn and they are stealing someone else's water, which is easily done by the addition or removal of a little dirt between the boundary walls or the diversion of water from a channel by the same means. This has been a chronic problem. According to the *Mukhiya* (headman), disputes over water have been the most frequent cause of contention in the village.

To turn to history. By 1929 agriculture had evidently caught up with irrigation, as indicated in the official report on Bihar and Orissa :

> Government was attacked [in the Legislative Council] for having done nothing to increase the number of Government irrigation works [Jagmohan, 1930:103].

The subject came up again in 1936 :

> One of Bihar's major problems is that of irrigation and in any scheme to increase the peasant's prosperity irrigation must have a prominent place [Wasi, 1938:101].

In order to use water, all the fields served by that channel have to be level and on the same plane to allow the water to flow. This means that leveling and lowering must keep pace with irrigation. Good soil thus removed is used to fill in low land or to replace bad soil. Sandy soil is carted off to town where it is sold to make concrete, among other things. Two men in the village regularly earned money by hauling sand to town, some of which they took without permission.

Where whole areas have to be levelled because they are too high or because they are unsuitable for agriculture, the land is leased to a brick company for a period of years, and a brick kiln is erected on the spot. Villagers have told the writer proudly that the Patna Medical College Hospital was made of bricks dug from village soil. Usually if it is only a plot or two which is being stripped, the owner will hire a brick-maker who will mold, stack, and fire the bricks on the spot. There they will stay until the owner has money and needs them to build an addition to his house or a new cowbarn.

As water became available in different parts of the village, double cropping has also advanced. The British government and the Indian government have taught the villagers the advantages of compost heaps, fertilizer, improved seeds, and crop rotation. These improvements have been adopted by the villagers to the extent that their education and means would allow.

From a cursory history of irrigation and land leveling given to the writer by the most knowledgeable man in the village, it is apparent agricultural production has increased significantly since the time of Phulia Devi. Furthermore, it is his impression that the rate of increase has been rising. During his stay he saw one new channel dug within the village and another one dug to make more direct access to the canal in order to increase the flow of water. Furthermore, the constant fights about water speak of the increased need for it. The places which have been levelled are impressive in area as is the constant activity of this type. The new agricultural production cannot be estimated and the man-land index does not take this into account.

Contrast the present-day quiet frenzy in agriculture to the picture of life in the early days given to the writer by the old men :

> The zamindar used to give the lands. Whatever he will give, he will give it in writing. There was no such thing as boundaries. After that the survey came; the survey was done and the boundaries were fixed. There were big, big plots. The boundaries were distant. The land was big. There were boundaries; everybody was satisfied, so there were no fights. If I have this much land; I can't plow this much; so let him plow ... but now in one plot there is ten divisions; now this one wants to encroach upon that one. ... At that time they had enough land, so why bother about more ? What will they do with it ?
>
> You leave it [land]; somebody else will take it; one leaves it; another takes it. Before the survey things were like that.

Sita Ram said :

> Previously they ate and drank milk, and wrestled; they were wrestlers. When they became short of money, they started selling milk for their clothes and food, and to pay the rent. Previously there was less yield; but now it has increased, rice, potatoes. Because of the canal, the yield has increased. When I am not doing well, and I have rice, milk and potatoes and I need clothes, then I will look for someone to buy milk. I have more than I need for eating; I want to sell some.*

Sita Ram's description reminded one of a Brueghel painting : peasants at their ease wrestling on the canal bank, drinking

---

*Said in English.

milk; herds of thirty to forty animals roaming the landscape; some farming and some selling milk and, most of all, plenty of time.

The decrease in herds was the inevitable result of the gradual shrinkage of grazing lands. The man-land ratio indicates the land was gradually approaching its carrying capacity. One middle-aged man told me that in his youth a villager would devote half of his acreage to cattle grazing and the other half to cultivation. Today there is hardly any land where cattle can graze freely; consequently, there are constant arguments over cattle trespass. In fact, Khagaul has a cattle jail, which has existed for a long time. When a man catches an animal grazing on his land he seizes it and takes it to the jail. The owner has to pay a fine to release the animal.

Most disputes, in one form or another, concern land. The writer has previously mentioned the diversion of irrigation water. In addition, people take over public paths for their own, build houses with less than the required space between them, move boundary walls between plots, and try to get another's land; or if they are strong enough, just occupy it. What was noticed in 1964 O'Malley saw in 1907.

> The most common class of crime, with the exception of thefts and burglaries ... consists of riots connected with land disputes or disputes arising out of cattle trespass and questions of irrigation [p. 163].

In an Indian village you do not fight alone; this explains the "riots" mentioned by O'Malley. A fight starts with two individuals, spreads to the two families, and usually, though not always, finally involves the extended families and unrelated families, which means full-fledged factionalism. Depending upon the circumstances, these factions rise and fall and become realigned in the course of time. This is just one example of how the economic is embedded in the social, for though the conflict is economic in origin it is played out along kinship lines. This conflict is due to a scarcity of land for growing crops — crops which they themselves consume. The current situation has its touch of irony : much of the land now fought over is the same bad land which the zamindar forced people to accept in the old days. It has acted as a reservoir, as a land bank, waiting for the time it would be needed.

In the absence of opportunities to purchase unoccupied land and to the determination of people to hold on to their land, the Roys had to connive continually to add to their holdings; money alone could not accomplish this. Sri Krishnu explained what he did to help his relatives get land :

> I said, all right, I will get it for you. If anyone wants to sell land here, then five men will go to buy it. Anyhow, I managed to buy land at a cheap price, and gave the money after buying the land. And so with a lot of trouble, I bought the land for him. If you want to sell land, and four people know it, you offer R. 500. The other man says R. 800; the man will forget the 500 and take the 800. And someone may offer 1000; then you forget the R. 800 and take the R. 1000 deal. You want to sell the land, so you take the R. 1000 offer, because it is up to you. That is why we bought it secretly. When the deal is completed, then we paid him the money. This is the way we bought the land.*

Sri Krishnu did not explain why the potential seller of the land kept this fact a secret. The writer knows, however, from the stories about the Roys that all sorts of pressures are brought to bear on the seller, including abduction and physical threats. Furthermore, as will be explained later on, factors other than price may be involved in the sale of land. (The significance of the word "secretly" in Sri Krishnu's statement will be treated in the analysis). Sri Krishnu dates his first participation in "parties" (factionalism), already in existence, from the time he repaid his father's mortgage in order to have it transferred to another man with the understanding that the new mortgagee would remove the present tenant and "give" the land to Sri Krishnu on a share-cropping basis. The other faction in the village, however, persuaded the mortgagee to go back on his word to Sri Krishnu and to give it instead to one of their men. Around 1935, Sri Krishnu was embroiled in another fight related to his right to cultivate

*Translated from Hindi.

canal company land. This, again, became a factional dispute. From the writer's observations, the pinch in land was beginning to be felt by the village in 1935. The many disputes over land in the last thirty years come in striking contrast to the peaceful relationships of early days when land was freely available.

One approximate measure of the increasing scarcity of land as time went by is the rise in the price of land combined with its relative immobility. The price has increased by approximately fifteen times in sixty years. The difficulties in ascertaining the rise in true market value through any time span are many. Plots are rarely transferred intact; they vary as to fertility; and in order to save transfer fees the parties to the transaction will record a figure below the actual selling price. To ascertain the rise in market value correctly, the yearly variation in the cost of living would have to be taken into account also. Yet there is value in the record as an indicator — along with the man-land index — of the rising trend in land values.

Since there is little turnover in land, price as a measure of value becomes inappropriate. Two changes in ownership of a particular plot since 1910 are rare; and it would be even rarer except for Partition which allowed more land to be sold when many Muslims fled to Pakistan. It was during this time that the village bought the bulk of its land. (This does not apply to the Roys who had their own way of acquiring lands). The inappropriateness of price as a measure of value in a peasant economy will be dealt with in the conclusions.

The trend towards crowding as shown by the man-land index is verified in a number of ways : a large number of disputes over land boundaries and land ownership, over cattle trespass, over water rights; the difficulty in buying and renting land (one man asked the writer to intercede for him with the Roys to obtain land to plow); the rise in the price of land, and the efforts to improve land; the population increase — all the subject of conversations in the village during the writer's stay there.

Contemporary British accounts concerning the shortage of land and the consequent shrinking of the grazing tracts both buttress this contention and place what happened to Phulia Tola well within a regional context :

> As cultivation advances the area of waste land available

for grazing steadily diminishes, and the prospects for the poor beasts are becoming worse rather than better [Hunter, 1886:519-20].

Nearly all the land available for pasturage ... has been given up to cultivation; and the cattle have to be content with the scanty herbage found in the arid fields or are stall-fed [O'Malley, 1907:102].

Prices [of cattle] have risen rapidly in recent years, owing mainly to extensions of cultivation on land that was formerly available for grazing [Moreland, 1912:120].

The pressure of the population on the soil in these areas [North Bihar] has reached its extreme limit, so that there is virtually no waste land left for the extension of cultivation [Lacy, 1928:85].

The difficulty of finding a solution of the [cattle] problem is increased in Bihar and Orissa by the almost complete absence of land which could be utilized for increasing the area available for pasture [Jackson, 1929:52].

An important milestone in the history and development of the village was the cadastral survey of 1910, which mapped and numbered all the plots, public and private, in the village. In that year the khātiyāns were drawn up; these listed all the plots plowed by a man or a family and in the latter case the shareholders as well. The legalities and intricacies of the various British Land Settlements need not detain us here (see James, 1914, for details), for we are interested in the practicality of the situation. While the common cultivator (*ryot*) could own land before 1910, it was only when the survey was made and the khātiyānas written that the ryot could prove ownership of specifically demarcated plots. The poor man, then, felt a measure of security about his acreage. The khātiyāns also made effective a law which had been on the books previously, though inoperative, that use of the land conferred ownership. A few people in Phulia Tola benefited by this. Moreover, as more and more land was turned to tillage, it became more and more important to have documentary evidence of ownership.

Although the transformation of grazing lands to tillage was inevitable, it was accelerated by the arrival of the Roys into the village. The village felt their entry in a way peculiar to its history.

Before their coming the villagers had been in the habit of grazing their cattle on lands belonging to Lachman Bhagat as well as those owned by outsiders. Lachman Bhagat himself was, because of his wealth, indifferent to this trespassing; the outsiders on the other hand, lacking unity among themselves and distant from their fields, were concerned but helpless to prevent it. The Roys succeeded eventually in acquiring most of the lands in the village which had originally belonged to Lachman Bhagat. At the same time the inability of the outsiders to protect their lands in Phulia Tola in the face of the antagonism and pugnacity of the villagers made them open to the overtures of the Roys to purchase their properties. In time, consequently, the land formerly owned by the Bhagats and the outsiders came into the possession of the Roys and constituted the bulk of their holdings. By 1946 the Roys owned so much land in Phulia Tola that they saw the necessity of joining themselves to their land. They, therefore, established their residence in Phulia Tola. The villagers soon felt the presence of the Roys, who took steps to effectively prevent the promiscuous use of their lands for grazing. Unlike the outsiders who had waged a losing battle against the villagers, the Roys were able to apply pressure on the villagers to accede to their demands. First, they were there to observe the trespassing and to complain; second, as members of the village and of the same caste and sub-caste, they were entitled to use the village legal machinery to punish trespassers; third, they had access to the courts when other methods failed. The fight in the cane fields was the culmination of these antagonisms.

The Roys, then, emerge as a distinct social entity in the village. They neither trespass on the property of others, nor do they allow others to trespass on theirs; the spirit of "live and let live" that was traditional among fellow villagers is alien to them. Neighboring villages, on the other hand, who were the beneficiaries of the anti-trespass policy of the Roys looked upon their actions as "civilizing" Phulia Tola. The process of "fencing in" of lands converted from grazing to tillage had been going on not only in Phulia Tola but throughout India for many years. The Roys' entrance into the village simply furnishes a dramatic example of this process.

As more land in Phulia Tola was put into production, less became available for grazing. Herds decreased and were forced more and more to graze in places which could not support a crop, so that today they can be seen nibbling on the grass along the sides of roads and paths, on the tops of the boundary walls, or pastured on the little high ground remaining. They are fed the chopped-up straw from the rice plants (which has little nutritional value), weeds, grasses gathered laboriously, tree leaves — all mixed with water. Years ago they were fed the milk left over from making ghee, but now the milk itself is all sold in the market. Some fodder is grown for cattle, and when the owner must, he buys fodder and oil cake to supplement the animal's diet. After a harvest, anyone has the right to graze his animals on the stubble, just as anyone has the right to weed anyone else's fields and keep the weeds. However, it is mostly in the fields of the Roy family where this — along with some stealing of the crop itself — is done. As a caste whose traditional occupation has been herding and milking, the Gowāllās have been most affected by the closing in of the land. Cattle trespass was a response, and Indian history had amply recorded this (O'Malley, 1907:50 ff., 164; James, 1914:12; Anon., 1914:12; Anon., 1924:7; Anon., 1926:50).

The agricultural economy of Phulia Tola is best described as that of subsistence agriculture. The term implies (1) production for consumption only, and (2) production on the level of mere subsistence. The mode of production is here called *house-holding*; the level of production is called *maintenance*. The type of agriculture which has always characterized the village is denominated *household agriculture*.[1] The concept of householding is central to the analysis.

Most of the crops grown in the village are consumed in the village. First and foremost of these is rice. The efforts at leveling land and providing irrigation had the purpose of growing rice, which is both the staple and preferred food. Presently, only two families sell rice; they are the Roys and Dharam's family, the second most wealthy in the village. At the other end of the scale, a few poor families must buy rice in the market. The other crops in the householding category are wheat, corn, gram, and garden vegetables. These are grown in soil unsuitable for rice or on rice land during the off season.

Within the last twelve years, potatoes, formerly grown in

1. Nash has made this same distinction (1966:22).

small quantities for home consumption, have been raised in large quantities for the market. The Patna area, however, has long been noted for its potatoes, which were widely marketed (O'Malley, 1907:99). Two years ago onions became a cash crop too. As land and water became available, rotation of crops throughout the year became possible. The Roys have been rotating their crops on land irrigated with an electrically driven tube well, the only one in the area.

Potatoes and onions are sold to men who come into the village when the crop is ready for harvest and estimate the amount of produce and bid on this basis. With potatoes, because the crop is underground, there is an added element of risk, and the few square yards which are uncovered are the only indication the broker has of the yield. The purchaser is responsible for the hiring of the crew of women to do the harvesting and the transportation to town of the potatoes. Sri Krishnu went into the potato contracting business two years ago; he claimed he was not making any money at it, but the writer, along with the rest of the village, suspect he was, for he was always drinking wine and gambling at cards.

In the case of Sri Krishnu's potato business and the Roy's dairy, there is a basis for estimating costs and profits, but as for business engaged in by the rest of the village in potatoes, onions, milk, cowdung cakes, and sugar cane, such estimates are difficult to arrive at since costs can seldom be ascertained accurately. The many *economic* uses of cattle in a household (Harris, 1965: 217-22; 1966:51-65) would require sophisticated accounting to assign costs to any one operation. Furthermore, it is the writer's contention that the sale of agricultural produce is peripheral to the householding economy. This includes the Roy family's sale of crops, on which they earn about R. 5,000 a year.

One may well ask why, then, would a villager raise and sell farm products, such as onions and milk, which yield no profit. (The Roys, who are familiar with Western market concepts, have never kept milch cows for their business for this very reason.) The answer is that in a householding economy the mere obtaining of cash is a problem. From the very beginning the village has always had need of cash — first and foremost, to buy the right to settle on the land and to pay its annual taxes and second, to buy things in the market; the sale of poppy, then milk, and now produce has provided the means. Selling of produce is not a matter of profit or loss but a means of converting goods to money. When large sums of money are needed, usually for weddings and funerals, however, only mortgaging or selling land will provide it; if the man mortgaging the land is poor, the chances are that he will eventually have to sell it.

Since the earliest days people have bought and sold in the market, and some have been employed there. People quoted prices of fifty years ago for rice, milk, clothes, etc. readily and with vehemence to show how the cost of living has risen. The payment for services involved in the *jajmani* relationships were made then, as now, in kind and in cash. The government has been mainly responsible for stimulating the use of money, for, as Habib concerning the Mughal period notes, "in most provinces the peasant was as a rule obliged to pay the revenue in cash," and, more specifically, "the peasant of Northern India, or, at least, of the central regions, paid his revenue in cash as early as the 13th century [1963:77, 236]." Thus the enduring need for money has forced the peasant to become a seller in the market. With the rise in the standard of living in the village, the need for money has increased.

Similarly, when, in the early history of the village, people had few material possessions, money was little needed, and that little was supplied by growing poppy for the opium factories in Khagaul and Patna (Choudhary, 1958:286). This crop was encouraged by the British, who supplied advance money for its cultivation. Thus poppy was the village's first and for a time only wholly cash crop. Some sugar cane was also grown to supply the mill at Bihta, which has existed at least since 1911 (James, 1914:24). Sugar cane, however, requires a year to grow and only the affluent could afford to cultivate it for the market. Most villagers in the past had their little patch of sugar cane to supply their own needs. Today, as in the past, only the affluent can afford to grow cane, and either they or the market supplies the villager's needs. What little milk came to the market in the past was sold by women for pocket money. The money Siphai's mother gave to him to buy the cream separator came from her milk money.

Before 1911 poppy was the chief cash crop of Phulia Tola. In that year an international agreement to cease the manufacture of opium, except on a limited scale, caused the opium factory in Patna to close down (Anon., 1912:xiv). The only cash crop which remained was milk. Consequently, from that time on milk became more important in the life of the village. Sita Ram's statement that they became short of money and started selling milk to enable them to purchase clothes and food and to pay the rent reflects this change in the role of milk, and, by implication, its new importance. We have here an example of an old element, the sale of milk, being intensified in order to replace a new one, the cultivation of poppy. Milk was to be one of the commodities principally responsible for the development of the higher standard of living of the village.

The writer has already detailed the story of the Roys, and a small group of their fellow Gowāllās in a similar position in the market. This section will be concerned with milk not as a business per se, not as a thing apart but as an adjunct, as something important and connected but in a subsidiary role to the rest of the village economy and wholly integrated with it.

The decrease in herds in Phulia Tola had been duplicated all over India (O'Malley, 1907:102; Lacy, 1928:85; Moreland, 1914:28; Hunter, 1886:519), and in part was responsible for a rise in the price of milk, both locally and regionally (Ghosal, 1946:298-300; Morsin, 1929:22). The people of the village remember in particular the spiraling of milk prices.

> The figure for ghi is interesting : it is well known that the price of this commodity has risen of late years owing to special causes [Moreland, 1917:820].

Moreland does not spell out the "special causes," but from his other writing, it is clear that one of them was the shortage of pasturage. The British government was forced to takc noticc of the problem in 1914-15 :

> The supply of pure milk to large towns engaged the attention of the Local Government during the year under review and was specially considered by a small conference of officials and non-officials held in Bankipore. ... It was generally agreed that the formation of co-operative societies of *Goalas* on the lines of that existing in Gaya constituted

> the most promising line of advance [Anon., 1916:52].

They also decided to encourage the growing of fodder crops (ibid.). The same year a cattle breeding farm was established in North Bihar (Anon., 1915:54). The choice of breeding milch cows or draft animals depended on how the herder — cultivator decided to use his land — whether for pasturage or tillage. The usual practice was gradually to convert land to tillage, to reduce but not eliminate the herds, and to graze cows and oxen on marginal land. The British, therefore, decided to breed both milch cows and draft animals. (None of the British or subsequent Indian solutions worked, for the supply of milk remains inadequate).

The herder-cultivator had another problem. The price of milk was rising, and he was unwilling to lose a good source of income. Having converted his best land to tillage, the milch cows and oxen were deprived of sufficient pasturage. Therefore cattle was allowed to trespass on neighboring properties. Such trespassing was the cause of many disputes for as less land became available for pasture, trespassing increased.

> The other factor in raising the price of milk was that the war has raised the standard of living and the demand for milk has increased owing to the growing populations in the centres of industrial activity [Anon., 1923:23].

The same report specified the places of supply and demand :

> There is considerable trade carried on in dairy districts like Shahabad, Saran and Muzaffarpur, in *ghee*, *dahi*, etc., which are manufactured in large quantities and shipped to Calcutta [ibid : 24].

These districts have one thing in common : they all border on the Patna District, the locale of this ethnology.

The volume of traffic in dairy products in 1921-22 is indicated by the fact that exports of ghee exceeded imports by 1,200,000 pounds in the district of Patna alone (Anon,. 1923b). This does not include rail traffic within Bihar and Orissa which amounted to close to half a million pounds (ibid.).

Owen, reporting in 1922, is quite impressed with the amount of business done in ghee :

> In 1914, 3,500 maunds of ghi were exported in that year by two Chapra dealers alone [Chapra being on the north bank of the Ganges, twenty-five miles west of Patna]. ... In 1912-13 ... imports of ghi into the provinces increased from 4,000 to 89,000 maunds [p. 57].

Since the Mughal period the price of ghee has risen so fast that it has become much more expensive than grains :

> In the Agra region ... butter, with rice, formed "the food of the common people" and there was no one in Agra who did not eat it. Similarly, butter was produced in such plenty in Bengal that besides being part of the diet of the masses, it was exported. In terms of wheat and millets it was considerably cheaper as compared with today. In the Ain it is rated 8.75 times dearer than wheat. ... As worked out by Moreland, the average price of *ghi* prevalent at Agra, Delhi and Lahore in 1910-12 was 13.9 times that of wheat, and it has remained about the same since then [Habib, 1963:53].

Narain estimates that from 1600 to 1927 the price of ghee increased by 17.5 times as compared to 10.8 times for wheat (1929:22). By 1912 the demand for ghee had caused its price to rise above the means of most people. Moreland notes that ghee was "used universally by the better classes for cooking purposes" and "exported in considerable quantities to the cities of Bombay and Calcutta [Moreland, 1912:1282]." During the first half of the twentieth century, peasants who kept dairy animals, especially — as in the case of Phulia Tola — when the expense of maintaining them was minimal, obviously greatly benefited from the steep rise in milk prices. The rise in the price of dairy products, however, did not benefit the lower classes, as Mukerjee observed :

> The most serious encroachment upon the standard of living ... comes from the virtual banishment of ghee and

> milk products from the dietary of the lower classes. Butter, oil, and sugar have tremendously increased in prices. ... Ghee and oil were much cheaper in Akbar's time relatively not merely to money but also to the food grains [Mukerjee, 194?:55].

The villagers estimated that since World War I the price of milk had risen twentyfold.

Concurrent with the decrease in the supply of milk caused by the decrease in pasturage, the demand for dairy products was stimulated by the presence of the British in India. The formation of an Indian bureaucracy by the English created a class of people prone to imitate English ways, including the eating of butter and the drinking of tea. The tea was drunk "English style" with milk. In Khagaul this bureaucracy was to be found in the Railway Colony, which had become important with the establishment there in 1929 of the railroad's divisional headquarters. The use of milk and butter was stimulated by the large numbers of English and Anglo-Indians who came from Bengal to take up jobs in the railroad complex at Khagaul. Some of the railroad officials became the valued customers of the Gowāllās of Phulia Tola. Travellers passing through bought butter at local shops and drank tea at the station. Tea drinking became popular all over India; in Khagaul it was systematically encouraged, starting in 1935, by giving away small packages of tea and serving it free from a tea stall set up for this purpose. The brewing of tea in village homes never became popular, but tea drinking at stalls finally caught on in 1937 when the attractiveness of the bazaar for the village men passing through on their way to work or to selling milk was enhanced by the installation of electric lights. Today sixty-one tea stalls in Greater Khagaul serve as centers for socializing. The social center of Phulia Tola has shifted from the village to two of these stalls. Any evening, early or late, and at certain times during the day, the men of the village will be found there exchanging gossip. The new class of butter eaters and tea drinkers added to the demand for milk and consequently caused the price to rise still further.

The price of milk attracted the landless poor to Phulia Tola.

One of the inhabitants described the situation :

> He came here, because he had no land, and he could start in business here in milk and curd. The city was nearby. The main cause was that my father had no brother or sister. He helped my father very much; my father told him to come here and start a business.*

The family brought him to the market; he hoped to return from the market with land.

As income from dairying rose, it produced for the Gowāllā caste and the village three synergistic results. In order to take maximum advantage of milk as a commodity, the villagers deprived themselves of milk as food — a food preferred by Gowāllās. They think that milk imparts strength to wrestlers, and their caste enjoys a great reputation as wrestlers. When the writer told a high minister in the state government, a Gowāllā, that he had heard that the minister had been a great wrestler in his days, the minister showed deep pleasure. For the Gowāllās to deny themselves milk — except for use as ceremonial feasts — meant that milk had become literally too valuable to drink.

At one time, moreover, it was usual for women to go to the market to sell milk and milk products and to keep the money thus obtained for incidentals. Nowadays it is considered bad form for a woman to go to the market for this purpose; men have taken over the job. About thirty years ago the participation of women in the market became the subject of heated controversy. Women engaged in selling milk had their clay jars smashed by Gowāllās from Phulia Tola. Ostensibly, the men were trying to improve their caste standing and by selling milk in the market the women were thwarting their efforts, for women selling commodities in the market was a mark of low-caste behavior. But the main reason why men took over an occupation long held by women was economic rather than social. For milk had become the principal cash crop and as such too important to leave in the hands of women. Men never take cowdung cakes to the market, as women do. Money from this source is considered pocket money as milk money was formerly. A sight which

*Translated from Hindi.

epitomized the situation was one the writer witnessed late every afternoon when the next door neighbor and his wife would set off to market, he with a pail full of milk in his hand and she with a basket of cowdung cakes on her head. The change in occupational roles demonstrates, once again, how the economic is embedded within the social.

As early as 1907 O'Malley called attention to the Gowāllā women who "go about selling milk, butter and *ghi* [p. 50]." In 1911 this situation still prevailed :

> The women of the artisan classes generally relieve their husbands of the lighter and simpler forms of labour ... the Goālā's wife sells the milk [Gatt, 1913:411].

But by 1921, just ten years later, we learn in the Bihar and Orissa section of the *Census of India* of a new and forceful attitude by Gowāllās :

> The men of this caste refused ... to permit their womenfolk to attend the markets to sell milk and *ghi* : this has on at least one occasion resulted in *temporarily disorganizing a bazaar* and in causing serious inconvenience to their neighbors [Tallents, 1923:23]. [Italics supplied.].

A report of the British secret police mentions the local area as the scene of agitation against women's participation in the market and notes the agitation was "being religiously carried out [Anon., 1912: # 274]." The period of the agitation against women selling in the market, 1912 to 1923, approximates the time of the cessation of poppy cultivations and the rise to prominence of milk in the market place. Though the agitation occurred within the social context of upcasting, clearly the economic factors were responsible for the substitution of men for women in the market. The declaration, however, that it was done for social reasons may reveal the existence of conscious and unconscious models (Levi-Strauss, 1953:526-27).

The contact of the village and the town through the years became closer. Coming into the market regularly to sell milk, men began to spend more time socializing there than in the village. As the milk trade became more important, increasing numbers of men were drawn to town. The bazaars with their crowds of people and shops and electric lights were attractions which added to the incentives of trade. People from the village would meet at the Roy dairy or at the tea stalls. Moreover, as men took jobs in town, they met new people and mingled with them socially, and the town became the center of much social activity. Today, for example, various departments in the railroad compete with each other in singing contests, with the merchants in town supplying the spices and cigarettes which are passed around on such occasions. The merchants also provide the images during the important religious holidays. People come in from the village to see them. In some ways Khagaul has become the capital of Phulia Tola.

Almost from the founding of the village, opportunities for outside employment have played a part in the economy and attractiveness of Phulia Tola; in recent years such opportunities have increased in number. At present fifty-two men work full or part time outside of the village. Two of the early settlers worked in Khagaul, one for Dr. Holmes, chief of the railraod hospital. This man was responsible for the presently oldest man in the village getting a job with Dr. Holmes. That man, in turn, brought in a relation of his from the village to help with the work of tending Dr. Holmes' cows and to do odd jobs, such as accompanying Dr. Holmes and his wife on a tiger-shooting expedition near the Nepal border. (With the money they earned, the two men bought land in Phulia Tola). Just as one man brought the other in to work with him, both men have been helped by British officials to get jobs for their sons in the railroad's electrical department. In turn other members of the families were subsequently employed in this same electrical department. Today the family of the second man who worked for Dr. Holmes is the second richest family in the village. It has for a long time been supplying the British with milk. This second man was also the one who told the writer that their British customers on being transferred out of Khagaul would make a gift of the unearned portion of the money which they had paid in advance. He credits much of his family's success to the influence of the British.

During the years various people have had jobs in Khagaul, Patna and Calcutta. All, except two brothers, gave up their jobs as soon as their condition improved or when they were needed in the village. The two brothers, who were the only family ever to move out of the village, decided to stay in Calcutta.

The largest single employer of people from Phulia Tola since 1956 was the Hydraulic Institute of Khagaul, situated just three-quarters of a mile north of the village, alongside the main canal. At the time of the writer's departure approximately twenty men in the village had full or part-time jobs with the Institute. He was asked to intercede with one of the high officials to get people jobs there. The number of men from the village who work there fluctuates from day to day; they are mainly day workers and are not reckoned among the permanent staff. The second largest employer is the railroad, and it does not hire temporary help.

Only a few men work outside the village at distances too great for them to commute. Of these only one man has taken his family with him. The others have their wives and children living with their extended families in the village. All these men, married or single, would prefer to live at home, for it *is* their home — the place where they were born, where their parents, brothers, wives and children live. The other man who lives and works outside the village would prefer to have his wife with him, but he cannot afford to do so.

For the man who works in town, especially the one who cannot commute, the advantages of living in a joint family are marked. As a member of a joint family, he has his share in the family lands and purse; if he is "separate," he must look after his land by himself. During the training and early stages of his job, especially if it is a sleep-away job, the family will have to contribute to his maintenance, for his salary will not suffice. As a member of a joint family, he is entitled to this. Later on he will be expected to contribute to the family's common purse from any surplus remaining after he fills his needs. The failure to contribute to the common purse becomes a cause for argument and sometimes leads to the breaking up of the joint family. Men who do wage labor lend a hand with the farming when they are off duty. Those distantly located get leave at times of plowing, planting, and harvesting. Even though the rent-free house on the out-skirts of Patna and the high salary which Ram Gopal Roy receives as Under-secretary of Local Self Government allow him to support himself easily, he still sends his car to the

Roy family house in the village at the end of every harvest season for such produce as his family needs, and he considers himself part of his joint family. When he retires, he plans to resume living in the village. At every important move, the family consults him; they also borrow his car frequently.

The question arises : Is the man who lives in the village, owns land in the village, and works at wage labor a part of the village economy or a part of the market economy ? Since none of the wage laborers can sustain himself by his earnings alone and is in some degree dependent on his share of the property, and since the mutual obligations of the man and his family remain the same, it is reasonable to conclude that the landowner who works at wage labor still belongs to the peasant economy. So long as a man's nutritional needs are met by his family's cultivation, his wage labor is similar to a cash crop, in that energy is being converted to money which is used to supplement the peasant economy but which does not alter the basic form of the peasant economy.

A few men have tried to establish businesses from time to time, but, with the exception of the Roy family and Sri Krishnu and his potato business, they have for various reasons been unsuccessful. One family had been doing well in a business similar to the Roys' but on a smaller scale until the government placed an embargo on rail shipments during the Hindu-Muslim riots. Three men earn a regular living from the hire of pony carts; two have gotten into the business only recently, but the third has been at it for over thirty years. Two men of the village regularly haul items by their ox-carts, sometimes for hire and ofttimes on their own initiative selling the unwanted dirt left over from land-leveling operations to people in town. Almost every family has an ox-cart and hires out its services on a catch-as-catch-can basis.

The salient characteristic of labor in a village household economy is the interchangeability of jobs for any one person in the family, synchronically or diachronically. Within the limits of physical capabilities and social customs, family members alternate, as need or personal whim dictates, in any job for the short or long term. On the same day a man in the village may farm, milk, and make two trips to Khagaul to deliver the milk. Each "occupation" supplements the other and is a necessary part of a whole. The man who used to be in charge of the dairy in Calcutta became the supervisor of the land when he had become old. Another man, who usually went neatly attired to his contracting business in town, took over the plowing when his older brother got sick. Reference has been made to the wage laborers who come home in the evening to work their fields, or rise early to tend them before going to work. India is predominantly a peasant economy whose essence is unity — the unity of occupations and of members of the family in the common cause of working and living together.

This "plurality of occupation" caused the British administrators great difficulties when they tried to classify the population by occupation. The problem was apparently a national one :

> Besides the difficulty of vagueness of definition, there was that of plurality of occupation. The system of classification which has been adapted is not altogether suitable for India [Bourdillon, 1883:168].

The following comments apply to the inhabitants of Phulia Tola who are Gowällās like the Ahir mentioned :

> Under this head [Raising Farm Stock] the decrease is accounted for by the increased numbers under group 123 which includes sellers of milk, butter, *ghi*, etc. It is difficult to say under which of these heads the occupation of the Ahir should more properly be classified [Tallents, 1923:257].*

Obviously the solution to the problem was to revise the occupational categories and such revisions the British made continually. They distinguished between primary and subsidiary occupations, and between principals and dependents. The last-named "are the children, the women and the old and infirm who have to look to others for their support, a worker being distinguished from a dependent by the fact that he or she helps to augment the family income [ibid.:249]." If you would apply this criterion to Phulia Tola, then all would be workers, except

*Ahir is another of the Gowāllā caste names.

the babes in arms, for women do a substantial amount of agricultural work while the old men and the children tend cattle. Even old Koli Bhagat would have to be included as a worker, for though his legs are so badly crippled that he literally drags himself from place to place, he nevertheless contributes to the family by chopping up hay for fodder.

A question that the British administrators were always asking was the following : Does a Gowāllā who milks, farms, and sells his milk in the same day cease to be a cultivator the moment he picks up his milk pail ? Suppose his cow dies. Has he then abandoned his caste calling and should he be dropped from the rolls of milk sellers ? In the tables of the Census of India, the British tried to solve the problem by apportioning the total number of the members of each caste according to the degree that caste occupation was followed — totally, partially, or not at all. This last classification was sub-divided according to occupation, including agriculture, which meant that the British recognized two important facts of Indian life : (1) the reality of "plurality of occupations," and (2) the overwhelming importance of agricultural life :

> The production of their own food-supply still constitutes the main occupation of the people. The vast majority of the people of the province are either directly engaged in or dependent on agriculture and many others pursue it as a subsidiary occupation; all these persons are directly interested in the outturn of the crops [Tallents, 1923:11-12].

Their model, however, of how an economy functions conceptually blinded them when it came to understanding Indian economic life. One of the chief characteristics of a market economy according to the leading economist of the day, Adam Smith, was the division and specialization of labor (Heilbroner, 1967:55-56; Dalton, 1968:3-4, 128). Thus the British tried valiantly to supply these same discrete categories of a market economy to the Indian situation. They failed to recognize that the family, not the individual, was the economic unit and that its base was agriculture.

Under a householding economy, furthermore, land cannot be assessed according to the values of a market economy. This fact was the cause of similar difficulties for the British when they assumed the powers formerly held by the Emperor and tried to decide "whether to regard land revenue as a rent or a tax [Neale, 1957:29]." The pattern of village economy simply did not fit in with the concepts of the market-oriented colonialists.

To return to the village. Since the early 1950's outside employment has increased and more emphasis has been placed upon it. To prepare for employment, families have encouraged their children to become educated. The lesson to be learned in the market was plain to see : the English had the best jobs, they were the best educated. One villager thus explained to the writer his motivation for going to school :

> My father said that now the time is coming for education. He was in contact with educated people. If you become educated, people will respect you. . . . He used to sell milk in Khagaul's residential area for officials. That's how he came in contact with educated officials.*

Another villager remarked on this subject : "If you get educated, you'll get a good job."* A third put it another way : "Besides learning, they sent me to school because it will improve my future."* Dhaneshwer Prasad Roy's statement in this connection is interesting : "They get the study only to improve their life."** Government service is preferred to private enterprise, for it offers greater security; for the same reason agriculture is preferred to cattle raising. Because it is associated with higher earnings, education becomes an important asset in a prospective mate — to a greater degree in a future husband, to a lesser degree in a future wife. Distinctions of academic degree are more highly refined than in the United States. For example, an Indian speaks of "matric (matriculated from high school) fail," "B.A. fail," and M.A. fail" just as readily as he will speak of "pass" in those categories. This means the person has completed all the work for that level but has failed the final examination. Thus an "M.A. fail" is higher than a "B.A. pass."

Money is needed to educate a child. Tuition and books must

---

*Translated from Hindi.

**Said in English.

be paid for and the child must be dressed in a fitting manner. Furthermore, if the child can do useful work tending cattle, working around the house or in the fields, his labor must be sacrificed. A common reason for not sending a child to school is that his labor is needed at home. Thus only the richer families can afford to educate their children, just as only they can afford to keep their women in the house (*purdah*). The wife of a poor man must work in the fields and go to market. Education and purdah contribute to a family's prestige and figure in marriage negotiations.

The sale of milk and wage labor have been the two factors responsible for the improvement of the standard of living in the village. Land is the single most important criterion of wealth in India. As mentioned above, the village land — excluding that owned by the Roys and another family who made a windfall profit when the government bought their land in Patna — has gained in acreage. And almost all land has been improved. The income from dairying made possible the purchase of land which was gradually converted from pasture to tillage. The rise of the standard of living can be observed also in the new dwellings and the materials from which they are constructed. Much is preserved from the past, but certain features are no longer in evidence. Thatch roofs, for example, have been replaced by roofs of tile. The newest buildings are made of brick with shuttered openings (resembling windows without glass) in contrast to the solid mud walls. Some homes have two stories; the Roy house has three. Bricks themselves have changed; in the past they were made in a round shape, now the form is rectangular. During the building season the writer witnessed eight houses in the process of being built or repaired with brick. Incidentally, the Roy house is the only one faced with cement, but behind the cement are brick walls cemented with mud.

A few families own chairs, benches, and tables; the last are used only for eating when some Western-oriented guest appears. Brass utensils are common, having replaced those made of clay. Kerosene lanterns and electric lights have taken the place of the small wick lights fed by a pool of oil from pressed seeds. Electricity came during the year the writer was there, and a few months after its introduction five families had electrical service. Others, who did not buy the service, would tap the lines for such occasions as weddings and song fests. (You will recall there were about eight electricians in the village). From the top of every house with electricity one naked electric light shone — a symbol of the owner's pride. One man, Sri Krisun, whose house had only one story, strung up a light on top of the electrical pole next to his wall. Two families bought radios which blared out Indian movie music most of the evening. Previously the Roys and another man had had a battery-operated radio.

Today there are many individually owned wells. Some of them are inside the courtyard, where women may bathe in private. Two families even have indoor latrines; the Roys have two — one inside for the women, and a double-enclosed one outside near the cowbarn. Forty families have a hay-cutting machine replacing a hand chopper. Over half of the families take their rice to town for grinding; the other half pound it by hand. Clay jars have disappeared; milk and water are now carried in pails.

About ten to fifteen years ago bicycles appeared in the village. Somewhat later watches started to adorn wrists, their principal use. Younger men wear Western-type clothes to work. Indian clothes are now of a better quality. Every woman has one or two good saris tucked away with her ornaments in a footlocker.

The *Report* of the *Census of India*, 1931, for Bihar and Orissa gives startling confirmation of the material changes the writer had observed in the village :

> By common consent there has been a marked rise in the general standard of living during the last ten years.... It is perhaps most apparent in the increasing use of articles which a short time back were regarded as being in the nature of luxuries [Lacey, 1933:70].

Lacey then goes on to list them. Lanterns replaced clay *dira* lights; kerosene was used instead of seed oil; the *dhoti* replaced loin cloth, metal utensils replaced those of clay, umbrellas replaced palm leaves, roof tiles replaced thatch; tailors used sewing machines; men discontinued wearing ornaments; wrist watches, pens, cot-type beds, standing wardrobes, tin footlockers, flashlights, bicycles, shirts,vests, and shoes came into use. All these changes might be observed in Phulia Tola.

The rise in the material standard of living of the villagers was matched by the adoption of higher social standards. Education and purdah were important but most important was a lavish expenditure for marriage celebrations. Martin, in charge of the census of 1921, underlines this fact in the following remark :

> It is not unusual for a family to live in comparative squalor and yet spend large sums on a marriage festival or a law suit [1921:54].

Indian marriages involve a complex of negotiation, bargaining, ceremony and ritual that brings into play, even at the village level, the many pulls and tensions of Indian social life.

When the parents decide that a boy or girl is ready for marriage, word is sent out along the network of relatives. The girl will have reached at least puberty and the family will be seeking a husband who is a few years older than the girl. The time for a boy to marry depends on how far along he is in school, for the tendency is to keep him unmarried while he attends school. But much is determined by the boy's ability and the finances of the family. The underlying reason for the stress on education is that the farther he goes, the higher the dowry he will get, for this is predicated on his potential earning capacity. Hence, educated boys are in demand. Since for the most part girls are not educated, this criterion does not apply to them; though if a girl is educated, it will be considered in calculating the dowry. A family with a highly educated boy will avoid an uneducated girl as beneath them. However, a larger-than-usual dowry also can compensate for this lack. A marriage will never be arranged where the girl is the more educated of the two. This becomes a problem for a family such as the Roys, who routinely send their girls through the seventh grade or higher. However, the problem is more apparent than real; only families who have sent their sons to college will be considered eligible by the Roys.

No matter what their wealth and position, the girl's family is always regarded as inferior to the boy's family. When a suitable male appears, five or more of her family must personally seek out his family. Before they do this, the *āgwā* (go-between) who is usually related to both sides and the one who has made the contact, will have already taken a look at the boy. He will have described the boy and reported on his family's wealth and position. Often someone from the girl's family will have also seen the boy in an informal situation. The boy's family will have also been apprised of the girl's appearance and of her family. When the two families meet, the dowry will be agreed upon and arrangements for the wedding ceremonies will be made. The girl's party may have to visit many villages before a marriage can be arranged, and, in a like manner, the boy's party may receive many offers of marriage. All these arrangements consume time.

If the discussions between the two families have gone well, the next step will be a formal visit to see the girl. The boy's party will travel to her home in their best clothes and be received with *nāsta* (snacks), spices, and small talk. Eventually they will be invited into the courtyard, where they will form into a semi-circle, and then the girl, in her best sari and with eyes turned to the ground, will be brought out. She will squat on the carpet, and the boy's party will ask her a few questions and, if the girl has been represented as being educated, request a demonstration of her reading and writing ability. All will then retire. If the boy's party is satisfied, they will perform the *chEkkha* (contract) by presenting gifts for the girl. Usually the girl's people will give their chEkkha for the boy at the same time; otherwise the ceremony will be performed at some other time, but never in a formal way. At none of these ceremonies is the boy present or allowed to see his future wife, although occasionally someone contrives to see his future wife before marriage.

The *tilak* ceremony is held a few days before the wedding; the girl's family accompanied by some friends and neighbors comes to the boy's house where he is presented with the dowry amid the proper religious ceremonies presided over by two pandits, usually one from each side. The dowry consists of cash and household goods and items for the boy himself, such as a watch, bicycle, and clothes. The money is counted publicly and the goods examined carefully. After this the guests and the village men are served a meal. Sometimes the village women are served too, but only later on after the other guests have departed. Only rich families such as the Roys invite all the men of the village as well as outsiders to their wedding feasts. At all weddings, however, at least one man from each family in the village is invited.

The wedding itself takes place in the bride's village. The

groom's party arrives in the early evening, with his people and the rest of the village, except for the bride's party, he is carried in a sedan chair triumphantly around the village. The party is accompanied by a band of musicians, men carrying high-intensity gas lanterns, and others throwing fire crackers. The boy stops briefly at the village altar and then retires to a designated place where his group is fed nāsta. His family will have arranged previously for a tent to be set up where their party will be entertained. At one point the groom's party presents gifts to the girl. Sometime during that first night the guests and the villagers will be served food. The bride's family and the groom's family each plays host to its own village.

Usually the groom's party will sleep overnight, feed itself breakfast, be fed lunch by the bride's family, and depart with the girl, placed in the sedan chair which originally carried the groom. The girl will stay with her husband's family for a few days and then return to her natal village. Some months later, there will be a second wedding, less elaborate and smaller than the first, after which the girl, together with the household goods, will return to her husband's house. The marriage is then considered consummated. In one instance in the village the girl had not gone to her husband's house after the first wedding but did so after the second wedding. It was explained to the writer that she had been too young to go the first time, and that in the past, when girls married at a young age, this had been the rule.

The degree of expenditure lavished upon marriage ceremonies depends upon the "capacity" of the families involved. Dowries can be large or small, the number of guests fed varies, as does the size of the band and the number of religious functionaries attending. In a rich family, the boy may arrive in a decorated car or, as with the Roys, be preceded by a procession of elephants. The whole affair may be over in one night, or the guests may linger for three days. Entertainment and the tent may be on an elaborate scale, or the guests may rent the community hall and pass out only spices and cigarettes. It all depends upon a man's capacity; the manner in which a wedding is celebrated establishes the family's degree of prestige.

The marriage complex, through the years, has changed. The marriages of fifty or sixty years ago contrast in their simplicity and their lack of pomp and pageant with the elaborate marriage ceremonies of today. Another contrast concerns the age of marriage. Ask anybody in the village above the age of forty at what age he was married, and by way of reply he will lower his palm to indicate that he was at the time a mere child. Today child marriage in the village is the exception and is frowned upon. As early as 1912 local Gowāllā caste conferences had passed resolutions stating that "marriages of minors should be discontinued [Anon., 1912: # 274]." The Census Commissioner also noted this about the Gowāllās in 1921 :

> The resolution of this sabha also are directed against ... child marriage [Tallents, 1923:236].

O'Malley mentions that "the Goalas in Bihar pronounced against child marriage [1932:175]." Later on he explains this as part of the general phenomenon of up-casting :

> The raising of the age of marriage among the higher castes from which the more highly educated are mostly drawn has had repercussions on the lower castes, which are generally anxious to assimilate their uses to those of their superiors as a means of enhancing their social prestige [ibid., 1941:236].

The villager concurs obviously when he says that in the days of child marriage they "were not so educated."*[1][2]

When child marriage prevailed, no one looked at the girl, for as many people told the writer with a smile, what was there to see ? Also there was no *chEkkha* (agreement to marry) for the girls, although then, as now, the boy had a *chEkkha.* Thus the new element is the formal visit to see the girl and her *chEkkha* while the boy's *chEkkha* has diminished in importance. This may be because of the increase in the dowry which is given during the *tilak* ceremony and which, in a way, has become the boy's *chEkkha.*

The writer was told that in the distant past the *pandit* and the Hājām (barber) arranged the marriages, but no one could actually remember such an occurrence; and the second oldest

*Said in English.

1. I am indebted to Prof. Theodore Wright, Jr. for stimulating me on this point.

man in the village, who was an orphan, is known to have arranged his own marriage. The belief that the Pandit and the Hājām arranged their marriage in the past may represent a tendency to raise their caste retroactively, like the putative relationship of Lord Krishna to their caste, for the higher castes used to have these functionaries arrange their marriages. Be that as it may, the speculation on the reason this custom changed brings forth the revealing conclusion : someone must have cheated and agreed to a marriage with a girl who had a physical defect. This fits in with the current fear of getting a girl who is not perfect. Many stories are told (and the writer knows of an actual case) of girls being married whose physical defects were not known to the boy's family. In one dramatic episode during a wedding in the village, the boy's party asked that the shawl covering the girl's head be pulled back (so that they could make sure that another girl had not been substituted). In a display of anger, her uncle made her do this, and get up and greet the boy's family besides. Remember, in the past no one even bothered to look at the girl before she was married, for this was a relatively unimportant matter. Today, however, when the marriage alliance is associated with wealth and social status, the girl's manner and appearance become matters of importance.

The villagers told the writer that the dowry represented the girl's share of the family property and in selecting a boy for the girl they are motivated by the desire to have her married as well as possible in order to insure her future well-being. If this were true then there should be some way of ascertaining the value of her family's property and hence the dowry. No method for doing this exists. Furthermore, if the girl's future happiness depends upon the size of the dowry, generosity should be the norm as in the case of gift-giving. The dowry would be offered and accepted in this spirit. Instead, hard bargaining is the rule, with the girl's father trying to give as little as he can. How much is wanted and how much can be given is known through intermediaries, but then comes the time for direct negotiations.

Mahasaji describes the process :

> My village men were sitting in a shop doing some business. My father-in-law, he asked them to arrange it. I

> will pay this much. They said, brother Mahasaji, you will give this much money; do it, and the girl is all right and is educated also. When I was going to arrange for my daughter's marriage, I went with a man to where the boy lived, saw the boy, talk's to the boy's party. How much do you want to give me your son. It was said by the man [who accompanied me]. You arrange it like this : you ask for this much. I can't pay you that much. He said, I will take 1200 — the boy's party. It was in my mind that no matter what he demands, I can give just this much. It was my own estimate, which I arrived at myself. I know I can manage only a certain amount of money myself, or I can get it someplace, just so I get it done. I will offer only that much. If I were not in a position and offered 5,000 or 10,000, then how could I do it ? I would lose prestige; so I'll just go. ... If you can only do 2,000 you will look for 2,000, and if you can't agree you'll go home. ... I will agree to as much as I can pay, from wherever I can get it : by mortgaging land, or selling bullocks, cows.*

The process is one of bargaining and as such displays the antagonism characteristic of buyers and sellers in the market.

The wealth of a family, usually measured by land; the education of its members, especially the prospective bridegroom; and its reputation and prestige — Ram Gopal Roy, because of his high position in the government, is always present as window dressing when his family receives important visitors — are the criteria for a family's entering into a marriage alliance. In negotiating the amount of a dowry, however, the parties will consider not only these criteria but also the arrangements made by a family in their own marriage settlements. After a year-and-a-half stay in the village even the writer could predict the approximate size of the dowry a particular family would offer and the type of wedding celebration that would follow, for it was always commensurate with the size of the dowry. Thus the dowry becomes an index of a family's status in the village.

---

*Said in Hindi.

A man's standard of living is part of his status and is taken into account when a dowry is negotiated. Dharam, the second richest man in the village, had received many groups seeking to arrange a marriage for his son who was a "matric fail," and hence highly educated and in view of his family's wealth especially desirable. Ram Chendra explained to the writer that Dharam wanted to get a dowry comparable to what the Roys received. Certainly he wanted to get more than R. 2000, which is what Kedar, head of the third richest family, had gotten. Then Ram Chendra added with distain : "Why should a man give R. 4,000 to those who go to the canal or road to defecate ?"* In the same vein, another man remarked : "Whenever someone comes, they have to sit at Kedar's verandah. Why should he give ?"* Clearly Dharam's mode of living was not befitting a man of wealth.

In the above statement, Mahasaji does not make clear how he arrives at the amount he can give, nor did repeated questions on this point elicit the information; he just knows. Several men whom the writer questioned concerning the rule to follow in establishing the amount of a dowry expressed it as follows : "up to a man's capacity,'* "according to a man's standard," or "to maintain your standard, you spend money." The one exception was Parmeshwer Roy, head of the Roy family, who replied immediately, "the profit of the dairy for a year." By this he meant to include the total wedding expense for a girl's marriage. Notice, only the dairy was mentioned; the income from the farm was excluded. Notice also that he was specific as to the amount and the source of the money in contrast to Mahasaji who was uncertain about where the money would come from and how the amount would be calculated.

Because of the proximity of the market, boys in Phulia Tola are desirable marriage partners than their country cousins, for it is felt that their opportunities for getting jobs are greater. This applies doubly for the boy who is well educated, for he will command a high dowry. Boys employed in the town or well advanced in school are more independent and ambitious than others and often ask their guardians to postpone arranging their marriages. Guardians of these boys are prone to listen, at least,

---

*Said in Hindi.

to the request. This situation has resulted in an innovation (dating back to about 1956) — the dowry for the boy. Heretofore, the only dowry was the one his family received. Occasionally a boy would get a cow as a gift after the wedding, but even this was used by the whole family. Now, through his father, the boy makes his own demands for personal possessions, such as a watch, bicycle, clothes, and so forth. This dowry becomes a new source of conflict weddings. The writer has seen boys at crucial moments refuse to continue with a ceremony unless this or that demand were met.

The new prosperity of the village has only accentuated the contention which normally develops as the boy's family invokes its traditional claim of superiority to exact maximum accretions to the bride's dowry even after the size of the dowry has in general terms been agreed upon.

In the preliminary stages of a marriage arrangement the two parties often fail to reach a full and firm agreement on the actual amount of the cash dowry. The boy's family will demand a specific sum; the girl's family will plead their inability to meet this sum and will offer a compromise. After pressing its demands unsuccessfully a number of times, the boy's family will declare its willingness to leave the matter to the generosity of the girl's family at the time of the actual ceremony. This declaration the girl's family will accept. For at this point each of the parties is confident that, in view of the small difference in amount separating them, the other will accede to its wishes rather than place obstacles in the way of the marriage. Each party knows that it is a social disgrace to stop the progress of a wedding once it has been arranged.

Sometimes the parties will come to an agreement on the amount of the cash dowry only as the result of compromise. This agreement, however, will not prevent each party at the time of the transfer of the dowry from resuming its original position. During a wedding ceremony which had been interrupted by a dispute concerning the dowry, the writer received confirmation of this attitude by way of a hypothetical situation he proposed to the member of an extended family of the bride. Suppose he wanted to buy a cow for R. 200, and the family member wanted to sell one for R. 400. After bargaining, they compromise at R. 300. The writer gives him R. 300 and receives the cow;

everybody is satisfied; no problems. "No," the family member replied, "I still want R. 400." Sometimes the bride's party will declare it has paid the full amount of the cash dowry by including the small series of token cash gifts given to the boy at various ceremonies which compose the total wedding ceremony, although none of these gifts had been mentioned at the time the dowry was agreed upon. The same contentions will arise on other matters concerning the boy's dowry, and the quantity and value of the gifts for the boy and the girl. Some detail usually becomes the subject of a dispute at the time of the wedding. Theoretically, the full amount of the dowry should be returned in the form of gifts to the bride. Actually, only 25 per cent of the specified amount is usually spent. This incites arguments. (The failure to arrive at a meeting of minds is common to everyday transactions in India.) Consequently, in every one of the ten or twelve weddings which the writer witnessed, some problem would come up, usually the dowry. It varied from grumbling to outright refusal to go on with the ceremony. On one occasion the boy's party refused to serve the girl's party until the issue was settled; at another time the groom's party refused to take the bride back to her husband's house, and persisted in their refusal months later. Usually the bride's party had not given as much as they had promised. The girl's party might complain that the groom's family demanded too much and the groom's family in turn might reply that they had to get what they give.

On the face of it, it would seem that by getting a dowry the boy's family is profiting; this is not so, for when you add up their expenses, both families spend about the same amounts on a wedding. The boy's family must feed its own village, pay for the transportation of themselves and their guests to and from the bride's village, provide breakfast for themselves, and supply the tent and the entertainment which takes place in the tent. They must also give the girl ornaments and clothes. There are other expenses which add up : the band, the sedan chair and its bearers, the fireworks and the lanterns. Each side pays its own religious functionaries.

The ostentatiousness of weddings today contrasts with their simplicity in the old days. According to some accounts the girl used to be brought to the boy's house by her family where a few ceremonies were performed by the pandit, some gifts exchanged and the guests fed. The guests would depart the same night, leaving the bride with her husband. There were no bands, entertainment, large feedings, overnight stays, and the dowry was just a token. Today, some fifty years later, dowries have risen to R. 2200 for the second richest family in the village and to triple that for the Roys.

People are of two minds about the high cost of weddings. On one hand, the amount of the dowry, the display, and the number of guests served are all matters of pride and prestige. The parties concerned will therefore always exaggerate these particulars in recounting a wedding. But one villager gave the other side of the coin :

> Everyone could earn bread for his own sake. There wasn't the dowry system then; therefore they didn't have to spend as much as they do now. ... We have to spend huge sums of money, which we really can't afford considering our financial position. But everyone wants to marry his daughter into a higher family. Because of this people get into trouble. People have always tried to marry their daughters into good families. It wasn't as much as today. They didn't have to give so much [in dowries]. They didn't have to spend money building houses or in education.*

The man was complaining about the higher standard of living, and in particular the high costs of getting their children married which he and others had been forced to bear.

His complaint, also, was directed against the recent emphasis on marriage age, the concern with a girl's physical appearance, the boy's earning capacity (actual or potential), the dowry, and the physical trappings of the marriage ceremonies. Marriage and wedding have become both the expression and the symbol of the effort towards higher social position. The *tilak* ceremony where the dowry is transferred and publicly counted is always crowded with people, for in this ceremony the family exhibits its status.

This explains the striving after higher dowries, the process of fixing the dowry by hard bargaining, and the ever-present

---

*Translated from Hindi.

antagonism characteristic of a market transaction. The boy and girl have become commodities in the market of social status. The writer was told, often, that the girl's family tries to get the "best" boy, meaning the one with the greatest prestige in his class. You cannot escape your class, but you can try to do the best within it. Marriage has become for the Gowāllās a mechanism for linking families of the same social level and validating changes in family fortunes. The dowry is the summation of a family's prestige. The steady increase in the size of the dowries of the Roy family through the years indicates not only *their* wealth but also their connections with wealthier families.

Incidentally, if it ever were true that the pandit and the hājām arranged marriages in the past, the reason for the change would be that marriage was now too important to be left to outsiders.

A funeral is the other major ceremonial expense a villager has to bear and, while it costs less than a wedding, is, because of its unexpected nature, burdensome for a poor man. As with a wedding, a funeral is a series of ceremonies involving religious functions culminating in a meal for the village and outside guests. Again, the number of people served depends upon the means of the bereaved family. The writer has no direct knowledge as to whether or not funeral customs have changed with time; however, Tallents informs us in 1921 that "the Ahirs have also reduced the thirty-days *sraddha* or funeral ceremony prescribed for the Sudras to the twelve days of the twice-born [1923:236]." (This is an example of a change in a ritualistic criterion in the process of upcasting among the Gowāllās).

The writer does know that people complain about the cost of weddings and funerals; they are the two things they will point to as the cause of poverty, for they have little to show for them when the ceremonies are over. But they feel helpless to change social custom. The cost of weddings has long been a problem. The local caste meeting of the Gowāllās in 1912 resolved to reduce the cost of marriage ceremonies (Anon., 1912: # 274), and one of the All-India caste conference of the Gowāllās passed a resolution limiting the amount of a dowry to R. 51. The resolution, however, has been ignored.

Finally, the raising of the Yādāvā caste (formerly Gowāllā and Ahir) from Sudra to Kshatriya rank, if only in their own eyes, is the mark of their new standard of living. Their material success has been responsible for their social success. This is represented by their efforts to upcaste themselves. The consistent relationship between upcasting and economic and social change is clear. Upcasting, nevertheless, was resisted on ritualistic grounds :

> In the district of Monghyr the caste movement among the Goalas causes a good deal of resentment among their Rajput and Babban landlords, to whom the wearing of the sacred thread by these tennants was most distasteful. ... The conditions in the neighboring district of Patna were similar [Anon., 1926:51].

Upcasting also had its economic effects :

> The main cause of dispute was with the zamindars, who had to some extent restricted the custom of free grazing and insisted on their right to labour and produce at privileged rates, to which the Goalas replied by restricting the outdoor employment of the womenfolk of their caste, and curtailing supplies [Anon., 1924:7].

Summary

Phase 1. 1857–1910

Land ownership becomes an actuality. Unlimited land is available for grazing. A small amount of milk is sold in Khagaul by women; the price of milk is low; almost all of it is consumed by the families. Some land is cultivated for household crops and for poppy, a cash crop. The population is small. A few men perform wage labor in neighboring Khagaul.

Phase 2. 1911–1940

Poppy cultivation is halted. Ample land is available for grazing. The market demand for milk is great and the price rises. Men replace women in bringing it to market. Milk now becomes a "cash crop". This is the time of optimum conditions for milk since the price is high and the people of the village have a plentiful supply and restrict home consumption. The population is increasing. Land starts to be improved, and the quantity of crops grown for consumption also increases. There are definitely more men working outside the village, one or two as far as Calcutta. More and better material possessions are seen in the village. Marriage ceremonies become elaborate. The movement for upcasting is in full swing.

Phase 3. 1940–1965

Land for grazing is severely curtailed; a new emphasis on increased agricultural production is present. Factions form. Milk supplies are limited, and milk itself now becomes a ceremonial food. More land is bought. The population expands considerably. The men of the village turn more and more to wage labor to supplement their livelihood. Education assumes a new importance. Potatoes and onions become cash crops. The standard of living continues to rise and brings with it more elaborate marriage ceremonies and richer dowries. The emphasis in upcasting shifts from ritual criteria to social reform.

The economic history of Phulia Tola reflects the common experience of peasants and peasant villages throughout India since the completion of the Suez Canal in 1869. Once the canal was opened and the Indian railroads built, Indian markets were linked to each other and to a world-wide market. Food grains, of particular importance to the ryot, gradually rose in price. As noted by Moreland, "more food was now grown in ordinary years than India could eat, because there was a market for the surplus abroad [1945:377]." Baines, writing on the scene a few years after the completion of the Suez Canal, felt that the general rise in food prices benefited the cultivator but hit the professional and artisan classes hard (Baines, 1893:42).

Lacey came to the same conclusion :

> There has in fact been no appreciable change since 1921 in the percentage of the total population which relies directly on agriculture for the means of subsistence. Yet in the face of all this the people of the province have multiplied and prospered, showing to all appearances a cheerful disregard for Malthus and his laws. But in truth the solution is not far to seek. ... From about 1917 the price of all commodities began to rise rapidly and continued to do so until about the time the last decade opened. Then they

> started to fall again ... *except* [for] *foodgrains.* Obviously the lot of the agriculturalist ... was an enviable one. That portion of the produce of his fields which he must set apart to pay his rent was smaller than before, and after feeding himself and his family he was in a position to realize good money from what still remained over and to purchase more with the proceeds [Lacey, 1933:72-73].

The prosperity of Phulia Tola differed from that of other villages only in that it derived from the marketing of dairy products rather than the cultivation of food grains. Phulia Tola thus was "object and sample," to use Arensberg's phrase (1965:7), of the prosperity which Indian villages were enjoying in the years preceding World War II.

Chapter V

CONCLUSIONS

Analysis of Concepts

The observations of fieldwork correlated with the historical data lead to the conclusion that the village, with the possible exception of one family, is composed of peasants practicing an economy and a way of life in which it is embedded that continues to maintain its integrity against the pressure of a market economy. To support this conclusion the writer has constructed a model of peasantry based on the concept of *householding* developed by Karl Polanyi but ultimately derived from Aristotle. This concept has been explained by Polanyi in the fllowing :

> *Householding* consists in production for one's own use. The Greeks called it *oeconomia*, the etymon of the word "economy." ... The practice of catering for the needs of one's household becomes a feature of economic life only on a more advanced level of agriculture; however, even then it has nothing in common either with the motive of gain or with the institution of markets. Its pattern is the closed group ... the principle was ... that of producing and storing for the satisfaction of the wants of the members of the group [1957a:53].

Householding is production for consumption by the producing unit, and it is a form of economy separate and apart from a market economy. In fact, Aristotle had already pointed out, as Polanyi notes, that householding can persevere in the face of peripheral contact with the market :

> Aristotle insists on production for use as against production for gain as the essence of householding proper; yet accessory production for the market need not, he argues, destroy the self-sufficiency of the household as long as the cash crop would also otherwise be raised on the farm for

> sustenance, as cattle or grain; the sale of the surpluses need not destroy the basis of householding. Only a genius of common sense could have maintained, as he did, that gain was a motive peculiar to production for the market, and that the money factor introduced a new element into the situation, yet nevertheless, as long as markets and money were mere accessories to an otherwise self-sufficient household, the principle of production for use could operate [ibid.:54].

The history of the village economy fits the above concept perfectly; first poppy, then milk was sold, not for profit but to get cash necessary to buy things in the market and to provide dowries.

In his first presentation Polanyi placed householding on the same level as other major economic forms :

> Whether the very different entities of the family or the settlement or the manor formed the self-sufficient unit, the principle was invariable the same. ... The principle is as broad in its application as either reciprocity or redistribution. The nature of the institutional nucleus is indifferent : it may be sex as with the patriarchal family, locality as with the village settlement, or political power as with the seigneurial manor. Nor does the internal organization of the group matter. It may be as despotic as the Roman *familia* or as democratic as the South Slav *zadruga*; as large as the great domains of the Carolingian magnates or as small as the average peasnt holding of Western Europe [ibid.:53].

It is significant that Polanyi considers peasant holdings small and, furthermore, that he designates the family as a householding entity.

Subsequently, Polanyi, by subsuming householding under redistribution and defining the household as "smaller than society," drastically reduced the scope of both *household* and *householding*. Furthermore, Polanyi narrowed the concept to predominantly family oriented units, including that of the peasant :

> Redistribution may also apply to a group smaller than society, such as the household or manor irrespective of the way in which the economy as a whole is integrated. The best known instances are the Central African *kraal*, the Hebrew patriarchal household, the Greek estate of Aristotle's time, the Roman *familia*, the medieval manor, or the typical large peasant household before the general marketing of grain. However, only under a comparatively advanced form of agricultural society is householding practicable, and the, fairly general. Before that, the widely spread "small family" is not economically instituted, except for some cooking of food; the use of pasture, land or cattle is still dominated by redistributive or reciprocative methods on a wider than family scale [1957b:254].

Polanyi, it will be noted, has revised his original concept by equating the household with the "small family". From the preceding reference to the Greek estate in Aristotle's time and from the discussion in another article, "Aristotle Discovers the Economy," in *Trade and Markets*, it is clear that Polanyi now saw the organizational basis of householding in the domestic family group :

> The economy — as the root of the word shows, a matter of the domestic household or *oikos* — concerns directly the relationship of the persons who make up the natural institution of the household. Not possession, but parents, offspring and slaves constitute it [ibid.:18].

This clarification also applies to householding as confirmed in the posthumous publication of Polanyi's last work, *Dahomey and the Slave Trade* :

> In primitive communities reciprocity occurs as a vital feature of the economy; in archaic economies redistribution from a center is widespread. On a smaller scale, the pattern of the livelihood of the peasant family is householding [1966:xx].

In his last book, also, Polanyi identifies what had been implicit all along in his formulation of householding : the political factor necessary to account for the arrangement of the activities of the domestic group *cum* family :

> The economic foundation of non-agricultural society is to be found in particular ecological balances. With agriculture land moves into a central position; livelihood and social organization are related to the agricultural setting, be it tribal or familial. The economic pattern in such societies is householding. The movement of goods is directed by the householder, who both allocates the labor of the household and apportions the food to be consumed. Hence, in regions of rainfall tillage the *oikos*, as the Greeks called the "house", becomes a permanent and fixed social institution. Aristotle said the *oikos* consisted of the family and the slaves. About five centuries earlier Hesiod had pictured it in a similar way [ibid.:70].

C. von Dietze, an economist, in the article "Peasantry" published in 1933 in the *Encyclopaedia of the Social Sciences* also arrived at the conclusion that householding was the essential ingredient in peasantry :

> Common to all the shifting meanings ... is a view of the peasant as a tiller of the soil to whom the land which he and his family work offers both a home and a living. Peasant economy in this broad sense is already found in the earliest stages of history of all non-nomadic societies. In this period the peasant household is dependent almost solely upon the product of its own labor, a self-sufficiency which in some remote regions it has preserved to the present time. Its core is the family [1957:48].

Von Dietze emphasizes the integrity of the peasant economy :

> Although the share of his own produce consumed by the peasant is still considerable, it is far from sufficient for his needs as a consumer, aside from his demand for productive equipment and supplies. Peasant economy has thus been forced into a mold of a business economy, but

> the peasant has not thereby become transformed into a typical capitalist entrepreneur [ibid.:50].
>
> The most noteworth [theory of the peasant] is that expounded by Chayanov, who holds that the peasant economy is a family unit explicable in terms of the consumption requirements of its members rather than a capitalist enterprise bent upon profit making [ibid.:52].

J. H. Boeke underlines the self-sufficiency of the household cultivator :

> Production by the eastern farmer does not aim primarily at profit-making but at satisfying personal needs, and these needs are determined partly by a man's social standing. ... Not exchange but rather self-maintenance is the basis of existence; *individual self-sufficiency* is the dominant idea, the unit being the family [1953:40, 41].

C. M. Arensberg's description of family economy on the small Irish farm, a pioneering work in community studies originally published in 1936, will serve as an example of what is here designated as "householding" :

> Nearly all he [the Irish countryman] raises he consumes at home; his family and his farm animals take the greater part of his produce. It is only his surplus and his annual crop of calves which break out of the circle of subsistence and in so doing bring him the only monetary income he receives [1959:39].
>
> . . . .
>
> On the small farm, the owner relies upon the united efforts of his family. The countryman's subsistence farming is a family economy in which all members of the family take part [ibid.:41].
>
> . . . .
>
> The countryside knows the farm as a unit. The farm shares the name of the family working with it. It is inalienably associated with them [ibid.:43].
>
> . . . .
>
> The controls in farm work ... are those of a social group —

> the family. The countryman at work is little concerned with the usual economic categories. He is a family man. He may be the shrewdest of traders and the best of farmers, but what gives him his occupational status, determines his pattern of work, provides his incentive, is a set of dispositions arising in the balanced interests and reciprocal obligations of the social group to which he belongs [ibid.: 60-61].

While the term "householding" has not been adopted by anthropologists generally, the concept is well accepted, being doubtlessly adumbrated in such expressions as "peasant economy," "subsistence economy," and "self-sufficient household," as the following examples show :

> The term peasant has primarily an economic referent. By a peasant economy one means a system of small-scale producers, with a simple technology and equipment, often relying primarily for their subsistence on what they themselves produce [Firth, 1951:87].
>
> A subsistence economy is one in which production and consumption are more or less direct, without intervening acts of exchange among producing units. In this sense there are virtually self-sufficient households, tribes, and societies [Nash, 1966:22].
>
> The most general thing about production organizations in primitive and peasant society is that they tend to be derivate. The social organization carrying out the making of goods or the tendering of services is dependent on and derived from other sets of social relations [ibid.:23].
>
> The product tends to be distributed not by a return to factors of production, for these are not clearly distinguished in peasant and primitive economic activity, but instead by a scheme dependent on social status and the claims it entails [ibid.:25].

Robert Redfield agrees with Firth that "one may ... use the word "peasant" for any society of small producers for their own consumption [1956:6] but, unlike Firth, he would exclude the hunters, fishers, and herders :

> I shall call peasants [those] who have, at the least, this in common: their agriculture is a livelihood and a way of life, not a business for profit [ibid.:27].

The distinction between peasants and farmers, originally made by Eric R. Wolf (ibid.), was further delineated by Redfield. In the following he emphasizes control of land as an essential peasantry :

> One sees a peasant as a man who is in effective control of a piece of land to which he has long been attached by ties of tradition and sentiment. The land and he are parts of one thing, one established body of relationships. This way of thinking does not require of the peasant that he own the land or that he have any particular form of tenure or any particular form of institutional relationship to the gentry or the townsman. ... A peasant community may be composed ... of tenants or even squatters on the land, if they have such control of the land as allows them to carry on a common and traditional way of life into which their agriculture intimately enters, but not as a business investment for profit [ibid.:27-28].

A second essential characteristic of peasantry Redfield derives from A. L. Kroeber, whose words he quotes :

> Peasants are definitely rural — yet live in relation to market towns; they form a class segment of a larger population which usually contains urban centers, sometimes metropolitan capitals. They constitute party societies with part-cultures [ibid.:29-30].

Kroeber, I would add, makes the following distinction between tribal and peasant populations :

> [Peasants] lack the isolation, the political autonomy, and the self-sufficiency of tribal populations; but their local units retain much of their old identity, integration, and attachment to soil and cults [1948:284].

In his latest writings on the peasant, Eric R. Wolf enlarges his distinction between peasant and farm economy by affirming Chayanov's position that peasantry is a special type of economy (1966:2, 14). In addition, he embraces the concept of householding :

> The peasant is at once an economic agent and the head of a household. His holding is *both an economic unit and a home.* The peasant unit is thus not merely a productive organization constituted of so many "hands" ready to labor in the fields; it is also a unit of consumption, containing as many mouths as there are workers. Moreover, it does not merely feed its members; it also supplies them with many other services [ibid.:13].

The theory of peasant economy developed by Chayanov was accepted (with reservations) by the economist von Dietze and the anthropologist Wolf. Polanyi independently formulated and articulated the concept of householding. Regardless of their differences in terms all four are in basic agreement on the essential character of peasant economy and the necessity of describing it in terms relevant to its own cultural matrix and as an entity operating under economic laws independent of the market, even under conditions where the two are in close proximity.

What is new in Wolf's analysis in his insistence that the larger entity to which the peasant is affiliated is a superior political power:

> Thus, it is the crystallization of executive power which serves to distinguish the primitive from the civilized, rather than whether or not such power controls are located in one kind of place or another. Not the city, but the state is the decisive criterion of civilization and it is the appearance of the state which marks the threshold of transition between food cultivators in general and peasants. Thus, it is only when a cultivator is integrated into a society with a state — that is, when the cultivator becomes subject to the demands and sanctions of power-holders outside his social stratum — that we can appropriately speak of peasantry [ibid.:11].

The asymmetrical power relations that govern in Phulia Tola are analogous to those described by Wolf in the case of a German peasant farm :

> There exist in more complex societies social relations which are symmetrical, but are based ... upon the exercise of power. This peasant [Mecklenburg] ... was subject to asymmetrical power relations which made a permanent charge on his production [ibid.:9].

The writer's investigations lead him to the same conclusion : peasantry obtains only when the householding cultivator is involved with power superior and external to himself and his fellows. The writer objects, however, to Wolf's exclusive identification of superior political power with the state.

Wolf's presentation is incomplete in several respects. He fails to explain the process by which the peasant becomes a creature of the market and, most important, the genesis of the superordinate-subordinate relationship. On the face of it, to postulate asymmetrical relationships does not seem convincing; the peasant must have gotten something in return for giving goods and services to the superior power, for he had means available to remedy one-sided exploitation; he could rebel, flee, or simply abandon agriculture as an occupation (Thorner, 1962:42; Habib, 1963:116-17, 324 passim). The *ryot* (cultivator) was not helpless in his relationship with his *zamindar* (landlord) :

> The ryot's only protection in the last resource was desertation. ... It was a powerful weapon, amounting in effect to a strike : without agricultural produce the zamindar could not hope to pay his own dues; and an oppressive zamindar would drive his tenants and ryots into the arms of less exacting employers [Ramsbotham, 1926:15].

If reciprocity is the basic mechanism of coherence in society, then a superior power is in itself a structural part of peasantry *and* produced by the very conditions of peasantry.

These deficiencies in Wolf's book stem from a lack of a unified structural model of the peasant. From this deficiency it follows that a processual approach — one where the model itself generates attributes and further structural relationships — cannot be developed. Instead of a definition, Wolf settles for an enumeration of characteristics, largely unrelated. These characteristics could have formed the elements of a definition.

The authorities quoted above seem to agree that the following attributes are central to any definition of the peasant :

1. He is a cultivator.
2. His goal is to raise enough for his own consumption.
3. His family is the unit of production.
4. Even if he sells something to the market, as he usually does, he is not an entrepreneur.
5. He is in a part-whole relationship with a larger society.

The peasant household is unique in that it encompasses within a single structure three functions — social, economic, and political. All of these functions, however, are exercised only by virtue of the primary kinship bond of affiliation that exists in the peasant household. The functions alone, it then becomes clear, do not completely identify the structure of a peasant household unless the primary organizing principle, householding, is taken into account. Householding, in general, is central to any definition of the peasant.[1]

The economic functions of the peasant household (householding) are to provide for production, distribution, and consumption of produce within the same domestic family unit. Typically, crops are cultivated for family consumption only. Householding as a form of agricultural economy makes it possible for the peasant family to maintain, preserve, and even strengthen its bonds of affiliation by assuring an adequate food supply to the domestic group. Cultivation allows for the storage of adequate supplies of food and the stability of the livelihood site. The security thus afforded permits the household to separate itself economically from the larger group.

The peasant economy is usually designated as "subsistence." The two differing significations of this word explain the form and operation of the peasant economy. The first meaning, the consumption of that which is grown, has already been applied

1. Some of the ideas about models presented here are the result of discussions with Prof. M. Klass.

to *householding*; the second one, existence of the basis of minimal consumption, to *maintenance*. The two meanings are connected in that maintenance is a condition which follows from householding. In a household unit the consumption team is identical with the production team — both identified with the family. The social organization of the peasant family which gives viability to its economic organization also serves to keep the factors of production and consumption in balance. Any change in one will result in a change in the other. Hence the householding economy makes for maintenance, or, as it is usually termed, self-sufficiency.

In order for householding to be viable political control must be exercised, both within the family and outside the family. Within the family such control is exercised by the head of the family who organizes production and distribution of the family's crops.

The family's claim to the exclusive use of certain lands, necessary for the stability of family ties, cannot, however, be maintained by the sole authority which the head of the family exercises. A superior authority is needed to confer title to the land and secure the family's economic base against depredations and encroachments. When the land of the family is demarcated and its tenure on the land guaranteed by a superior authority, the identity of the family with its lands becomes complete. In India such superior authority is held by an overlord. In return for the security which the overlord provides, the peasant family must assume certain obligations. These usually take the form of either tithe or service or both. The reciprocal relationship between the household and the overlord, the larger political entity, is the second element in the definition of peasantry.

In exchange for granting title and protection, the overlord receives tribute or taxes from those he guards. Security is exchanged for tithe. Thus the peasant does not stand alone but is in part-whole relationship with this supra-authority. Paradoxically the same process which allows the peasant to form an independent household also inexorably binds him to that process. The tax collector coming to the village is the symbol of the peasant's part-whole relationship.

The reciprocal relationship of lord and peasant forms the primary avenue of contact of the peasant with the great tradition. If the lord wants his tribute in cash, then the peasant is impelled to go to market (in person or through an agent who may come into the village) to exchange his grain for coin of the realm; this forms a secondary connection with the great tradition. While the influence of town and bazaar is more visible than the influence of the supra-authority, the peasant's motivation for entry into the market is political, not economic. Von Dietze supports this argument historically :

> European peasant economy has not been entirely self-sufficient for some centuries. Where money payments to the lord of the manor or to some other overlord displaced payments in kind, money income had to be found through the sale of produce [1958:50] .

The peasant's tie with the larger entity is primarily political; there is, however, a concomitant economic connection.

Householding taken by itself tends to be static. The model of the peasant, however, is a dynamic one, subject to process and change; but it should be noted that the dynamism derives for the most part from the second criterion of the definition, the part-whole relationship. If change comes, it will be from the peasant's connection with the outside world. As previously noted, this connection is primarily a political one and can lead to participation in the market. Once the peasant is in regular contact with the market, he is susceptible to change by what he sees and by those whom he meets. In the market novel ideas as well as new goods may be exchanged. The market and the policy are the potential sources of innovation for the peasant. Thus, while the foundation of the model, householding, is static in itself, the derived conditions which flow from and complete it create a path from the outside along which innovation may travel. Certain types of innovation, such as a reliance on wages, can convert the peasant into something else.

The principles which govern the operation of a peasant economy differ from those of a market economy. The basic assumption of the latter is that economic values are divorced from human values. The case of the peasant is otherwise : his economy is his way of life. Not only is a peasant economy unlike a market economy, but when the two are in contact with one another, as in the situation under review, the peasant economy is inimical to the operation of a market economy.

In order for a market economy to exist, land, labor, and money must become "fictitious commodities" in that they must be organized into markets and be responsive to the market mechanisms of supply and demand (Polanyi, 1957a:68-76). But non-market-oriented cultures pose a problem to a Western economic system :

> If one were to attempt a one-word summary of the institutional requirements of economic development, that word would be *mobility*. Property rights, consumer goods, and laborers must be freed from traditional bonds and restraints, from aristocratic traditions, quasi-feudal arrangements, paternalistic and other multibonded relations [Moore, 1965:31-32] .

Householding is an example, par excellence, of an economy with "traditional bonds and restraints" which prevents the mobility of land, labor and capital. These three classical elements of a market economy are not commodities in a household economy, for they do not automatically respond to the stimulus of a market.

Furthermore, in a market economy land, labor, and capital can be analyzed separately; in a peasant economy the essence of householding is the unity of these factors.

Failing to recognize this unity in Indian life, the British produced unsatisfactory occupational statistics. Their statistics were focused on the individual, rather than, as it should have been in a peasant society, on the household. Consequently, they misunderstood the reluctance of the vast majority of the population to leave entirely the security afforded by agriculture for the uncertainties of wage labor :

> A large part of the labour troubles in the country is ... that the labourer will only work sufficiently to maintain himself and his family at the lowest standard, and the slackness of agriculture ... is the result of low rents which enable the cultivator, with a minimum of effort, to produce sufficient to support his family at a standard which he is too backward and unenterprising to attempt to improve [Martin, 1921:54].

The mechanism of the unsuspected peasant economy was interfering with the self-regulating market economy. Boeke has noted that in an economy which he calls self-maintenance and which here is termed household — in such an economy labor does not enter freely into the market place, for as soon as the laborer has earned enough to supply the deficiencies of his normal agrarian existence will he leave his job. In fact, the higher the wage, the sooner he quits (1953:40). (It was ironic to hear the Roy family complain when they had trouble getting farm laborers that the people of Bihar were the laziest in India; they were echoing Martin). Martin was looking at a peasant economy and its concomitant cultural values through Western, market-oriented eyes and judging it by the values of his own culture. The problem was one of different economies, differently instituted. His bias so blinded him to the peasant's values that he saw a contradiction when Indians live "in comparative squalor and yet spend large sums on a marriage festival or a law suit [ibid.]. But there is no contradiction. Law suits and marriage festivals are very much a part of their standard of living and give evidence of something above "the lowest standard" of living. To the people of Phulia Tola a wedding is the symbol of a family's standard of living. We see a similar bias in American society when the middle class objects to poor people spending their money on "frivolous" things. It may be that the law suits referred to had to do with disputes about land. The British solved the problem of an adequate supply of labor in some parts of Africa by imposing head and hut taxes which had to be paid in cash, thus forcing people into the labor market (Manners, 1965:220). Such a solution is implicit in Martin's statement.

In his article "Labour in Early Nineteenth Century Bihar," Ghosal depicts the conflict between the two economies and the triumph of one of them :

> Between 1800 and 1833 the wages of journeymen weavers and agricultural labourers rose considerably. ... Moreover, the great increase in the price of agricultural labor between 1813 and 1833 may appear rather surprising in view of the fact that these years saw the rapid decline of the cotton industry and the consequent unemployment of numerous industrial workers, many of whom joined the

> ranks of agricultural labourers. ... The demand for agricultural labor increased too, owing to the enormous expansion of raw silk, opium and indigo cultivations in these provinces. But a more important explanation may be offered, namely, that the purchasing power of money declined very much after 1813. ... The comparative dearth of free non-agricultural labour in Bihar during the period under review has been referred to in the works of Buchanan Hamilton, as also in some of the Company's records of the time. ... The main reason why in spite of the decline of the cotton industry the shortage of non-agricultural labour continued was probably this — that the industrial workers, who became unemployed as a result of it mostly fell on land, *preferring* to be employed in fields whether belonging to themselves or to others [1946:100-101]. [My emphasis—L.S.].

In the situation which Ghosal noted, the market mechanisms failed to produce an adequate supply of labor. The demand for labor had increased; consequently, the wages had increased; but the supply of labor was not forthcoming. The reason for the failure of the market economy is contained in Ghosal's word "preferring"; labor had an alternative to the market economy — a household economy. Labor chose to become peasantry. In Ghosal's words, "the industrial workers ... fell on land." There is also an indication that the workers tried the market economy and found it wanting. Agriculture gave security.

It is true that the system of *jajmani* relationships in India also restricts a free labor market but this fact is incidental to the present analysis.

The data reveal that the movement to householding was an unmistakable India-wide phenomena. In 1922, Owen estimated that "over 90 per cent of the population is directly dependent on agriculture ... the great bulk of the population is ... engaged in agriculture as its only means of livelihood. A further characteristic of Bihar and Orissa, as of India as a whole, is the predominance of the small peasant proprietor. The soil is divided and sub-divided into small holdings, the produce from which is barely sufficient to support a single family [Owen, 1922:49]." This report gives clear evidence of householding. Much earlier O'Malley had also noted its presence :

> For cultivators ... holdings are generally sufficient for their maintenance [O'Malley, 1907:129-130] .

In general, what had started the movement to the land is not clear. Demands of free labor (*begar*) and the flooding of the Ganges were some of the specific reasons the villagers gave for leaving their former abodes. Other reasons commonly cited in the area are the desire to escape oppressive rents or the threats of disease (Tallents, 1923:237; Habib, 1963:117). In the past zamindars have forced or induced, as was the case in Phulia Tola, migration to empty lands in order to produce revenue on them. The important factors, however, were those which "pulled" people to Phulia Tola — the fertility and availability of the soil and the proximity of the market. They came, in their own words, "to eat and to earn," meaning to grow crops and to sell to the market.

The official British reports attribute the extensi on and intensification of agriculture to population pressure.

> Expansion of the population forces the population to enhance the food resources by increasing the productivity of the tract [Martin, 1921:50].
>
> Cultivation is increased by increasing population, for the ryots must work to live [Firminger, 1917:697].
>
> A largely increased population has caused pressure on the soil [O'Malley, 1941:384].
>
> The pressure of the population on the soil in these areas has reached its extreme limit [Lacey, 1928:85].

The population causes more land to be cultivated, which causes an increase of population, which in turn causes more pressure on the soil. One might justifiably reverse the stated cause and effect : improvement in agricultural techniques and more extensive cultivation could have led to an increase in population.[1] Improved health measures and famine relief-measures which the British initiated — do not change the

1. I thank Prof. Andrew L. March for his skepticism about population pressure, which caused me to re-examine my thinking.

inescapable fact that in a country whose population depended principally upon agriculture for a livelihood, and which for most of its history since the completion of the Suez Canal has been exporting grain — in such a country the yield must have been more than sufficient to support its population. Be that as it may, the situation in Phulia Tola was clear. During the early history of the village the land was sought for grazing and cultivation and little thought was given to monetary gain, which the market alone made possible. During the early days of the village the market was relatively unimportant and was an unimportant factor in the economy of the village. It is true that even from earliest days the villagers maintained some contact with the market mainly through the sale of milk and poppy. For a long time the sale of milk remained in the hands of the village women whose earning provided pocket money with which they purchased commodities in town.

As the price of milk rose, however, the prospects of substantial income from the sale of milk raised it to such economic importance that this activity was taken over completely by the men of the village and ultimately transformed the character of the village economy. This development attracted increasing numbers of immigrants, all with the immediate object of acquiring cows and selling milk and accumulating enough to purchase land ultimately and settle down as cultivators. As these aims were realized, more and more land was converted from grazing to tillage. This conversion created a problem for the owners of herds since pasturage was restricted. The result — all over India — was the shrinkage in the supply of milk and a consequent rise in price. The prospects of a greater income for the sale of milk continued, however, to attract immigrants.

In terms of the environment, the development of the village has caused a change in ecological niches.

At first the two ecological niches of cultivation and herding complemented each other. This was the condition in Phulia Tola at the time of Phulia Devi. "With a given soil quality, technology, and crop assemblage there is an optimum size of farm that one man can till [Aschmann, loc. cit.]." When the amount of land exceeded a man's grasp, herding was the most effective way of extending that grasp (ibid.). As the population of the village grew through immigration and natural increase, the man-land ratio changed and with it the balance between agriculture and herding. At some point the population became large enough to make agriculture the most efficient form of energy capture, capable of supporting more people than herding (ibid.). Then as agriculture and herding came to compete, herding lost out—in Phulia Tola as well as elsewhere :

> The cattle have to be content with the scanty herbage found in the arid fields or are stall-fed on chopped straw, maize stalks, and occasional linseed [O'Malley, 1907:102].

Cattle were forced to find pasturage further and further away from the village or along the byways of the village as plots were converted to cultivation. The extension of irrigation and the leveling and filling in of land was the physical expression of the change from herding to agriculture, just as competition for ecological niches manifested itself in cattle trespasses against neighbor and outsider alike. So many complaints of cattle trespass arose that the authorities established a cattle jail where plaintiffs might leave an offending animal until claimed by its owner. The sale of milk as a means of obtaining land for cultivation was responsible for the change in ecological niches.

From the earliest times up to the present cattle have occupied their own ecological niche; they have not competed with the Indian peasant for food. Today, when agriculture dominates cattle grazing, keeping cattle remains the most efficient means of energy capture within their new, restricted ecological niche because the cattle are fed on what is unfit for human consumption (Harris, 1965:217-228). The efficiency of this system in the adjoining province of Uttar Pradesh was noted by a competent British observer as early as 1912 :

> The bulk of the food of cattle comes from the parts of plants which are not required for human consumption [Moreland, 1912:122].

(Moreland's remarks help date the curtailment of the grazing lands. The writer's investigations indicate that the shortage of grazing lands was felt in Phulia Tola about twenty years later). In the days when the population was small and barren land abundant, grazing cattle was the most efficient way of utilizing land and labor. In that period milk was consumed by the household and cows were therefore an important adjunct to householding; today this is no longer the case : milk is sold in the market to provide an "extra" income, but without altering the basic pattern of householding. In all periods the oxen used for plowing the fields have been an essential means of production for the household. Moreover, the ecological efficiency of cattle, whether as cows or oxen, has been implemented by the efficient use of family labor, for in the peasant family children and old men are assigned the task of caring for cattle.

In a figurative sense the rules of inheritance in Phulia Tola — males are coparceners and females receive dowries as their share of the family property — assign the males their role in life as cultivators of their own land. The result of this is an integration of land and labor, a condition which impedes their entering the market freely. Furthermore, there are hindrances to the sale of any one man's share of the property, for first he must get the consent of the other coparceners to divide it. If permission is refused, he does have recourse to the panchayat or the courts. While it is true that sons can ask for the division of the land and property, the village recognizes the right of a father to refuse for sufficient cause — to provide, for example for the future marriage of a daughter or for the care and education of young children. Besides being shareholders, males are part of the production and consumption unit. As such they resist division of the property, for it results in economic disadvantages. Separation means separate kitchens, separate dwellings, separate plots with the loss of the land used to form the new boundaries, and a separate labor force for each nuclear family. The viability of a joint family will be weakened by separation; some or all of the resultant units may not be capable of supporting themselves as householding entities. The joint family and its property is therefore held together by a common interest in production and consumption. In fact, it appears from casual observation that the richer the family, the more likely it is to remain joined. Thus for economic reasons the joint family is the ideal, though separation is viewed as an ordinary and inevitable occurrence.

By incorporating into itself the newer elements of cash crops and wage labor the household has remained the important socio-economic unit. Ram Gopal, the Roy family member who is a government official and who lives in town, explained to the writer the advantages of the joint family, particularly the division of labor which it makes possible :

> It is necessitated by social and economic reasons. By keeping together we add to our social prestige and also to our economic advantage. One gentleman looks after agriculture; other looks after some business; somebody takes to service, and such things. But suppose if you are partitioned : I have to look to my service, and then if there is fragmentation of holdings, management becomes costlier. ... Suppose if I fall in evil days, there will be others to come to my support. *But this joint family system operates only when there are properties to be managed.** [My emphasis — L.S.].

We already know that the Roy family found the joint family system well adapted to their various enterprises; to a lesser extent this type of specialization of labor is true of many families, especially, as Ram Gopal has indicated, since the advent of extra-village activities.

The very conditions for the maintenance of the base of the household economy make for flexibility in its operation. The undemanding schedule of tending land allows time for other work. Thus a man who works in town during the day can come back to the village in the evening and within seasonal limitations work in the fields. Anytime he wants to farm, he is earning his livelihood. This explains the variety of jobs which a cultivator can attend to. He can go to the market twice a day or even hold a full-time service job, and still take care of his fields. Thus the agricultural base of householding becomes more efficient when combined with cash sales and wage labor. And this explains the easy adaptability of householding to the market, whether in commodities or labor.

Because the family and the economical unit is identical, with all contributing to and sharing in the same kitchen and purse, the household has a community of interest, where everyone does

*Said in English.

what he can wherever he can. Wage labor has been adapted to the household on the same basis of contributing to the common purse and receiving from it as need demands. When the reality differs from this ideal, through withholding of effort or money, or taking too much, the family is in danger of separating. From the unity of the household comes the efficiency of its labor force. Ideally, the only specialization is service to the household; occupational categories are submerged in the total round of activities which make up the life of the peasant.

All of the afrorementioned items contribute to the continuation of the household economy in the village; its presence, in turn, hinders the functioning of the market economy.

Land in the village does not respond to market incentives of higher prices. Again, as with labor, if the economy here described were a true-price-making, self-regulating one, the higher the price, the more land available for purchase. But this does not happen, because price is not related to potential profit but to the demands of householding. The true cause of the fluctuations in the price of land in a peasant economy is the change in the density of the population supported by that land. "Thus", as Kerblay commenting on Chayanov states, "the state of the market is not a determining factor as in the case of capitalized rent [Chayanov, 1966:liii]."

The system of householding actually keeps land off the market. Households grow crops for their own consumption; the value of the land lies in its being the *sine qua non* of peasant existence. Therefore, the possibility of selling the land at a profit is never considered. If he has enough land, the peasant is secure, and, as C. E. Ayres says, the desire for security is the key to much of man's activities (1966:168). Cultivation is a skill which is easily learned as part of the process of growing up in an agricultural community. It is a way of utilizing labor which otherwise might produce nothing for lack of a market. A man who cultivates is limited only by the amount of land he has and his physical strength. Furthermore, cultivation is a way of directly converting ability and energy into food without the interference of others. When you eat what you grow, you are dependent upon nature but not upon the fluctuations of the market. Without land food must be purchased or bartered for a commodity, a service, or a skill. But these require the individual to make an investment or acquire some education, and even then he remains at the mercy of the market. Villagers, therefore, prefer cultivation to herding, for it is less risky. We have already heard the oldest member of the Roy family express the same view : "We purchase land to get food. ... We have not so interest in dairy than land."*

Thus even the wealthy Roys demonstrate traditional peasant attitudes in their reliance on land to safeguard their security.

In 1910-11 there was an important change in regard to land : the British government gave ownership of land to those who actually plowed it. This removed the peasant from the arbitrary rule of the zamindar and substituted for it due process in law. Now only a British court could remove the peasant from his land. This meant, in terms of the model, that the base of householding had become more secure. The peasant's vested interest in the land was buttressed by the law.

In a situation such as we find in Phulia Tola, where land, for whatever the reason, has become scarce, the peasant holds on to his holdings that much tighter, for he cannot replace them once it is gone. But the more he clings to it, the less available land becomes. This is the reason that, to gct land, secrecy, conniving, fraud and force are resorted to. These tactics alone restrict the mechanism of a true price-making market in land to the point of nullifying it. In this regard secrecy deserves special mention. The very lack of a free flow of information concerning land available for sale (as evidenced by Sri Krishun's statement : "That is why we bought it secretly") impedes the operation of a true market in land. If it were an ordinary commodity, and not the base of the peasant's householding existence, price alone would be sufficient to call forth an adequate supply of land. For the same reason householding can restrict demand. When some peasants in Madras were offered, hypothetically, as much land as they wanted, "their demands were calculated solely on the basis of the family's consumption requirements [Nair, 1961:31]."

We already know that the Roy family shares this attitude towards land with the rest of the village. Parmeshwer Roy, head of the family and a man who prided himself on being a businessman, confirmed this when the writer asked him pointedly,

---

*Said in English.

"Would you buy land today, if you know it would decrease in price tomorrow ?" He instantly answered yes, but would give no explanation for his answer.

The joint family in a peasant village exerts a powerful influence in binding land to a peasant economy. The joint family provides economic advantages ideal for the Indian peasant's way of life. The community of interests of the family members exerts a restraining influence on any one member selling his share of the land. In addition, the transmission of the share is not just a matter of right. If the village judges that the father has a valid reason for holding the land together, division of the property will be denied. There are instances in the village of sons who have left their families and who still do not possess their inheritance. Incidentally, when a family separates, the rest of the village is secretly glad, for land then may become available for purchase. Obviously, such relationships impede the free marketing of land.

"Price-making markets are integrative only in that they are linked up in a system which tends to spread the effect of prices to markets other than those directly affected [Polanyi, 1957b: 255]." The price of village lands tends to reflect the price of land in the general area, but in an important way lands within the circumference of the village are distinct entities. Land which is used for householding must be within walking distance of the peasant's home in order for him to work it and guard it against the encroachments of others. There is a familiar saying among the villagers : "The sandy land which is near your house is gold, but the gold which is far from your home is sand." Only people who live in the locality are acquainted with the particulars concerning soil fertility, drainage, and irrigation facilities; hence only local people are able to know the potential yield of any piece of land. The man who rents out land distant from his own village on a sharecropping basis runs the risk that his tenant will not take proper care of it and will steal some of its produce from him before division of the crop. For this reason land is generally bought by people of the area. Factors militating against strictly local markets in land are the overlapping of holdings and the system of having relatives take care of land distant from the owner's residence. These factors tend to produce uniform fluctuations in the price of land from one area to another; yet, here again, the basic factor determining the price fluctuations are the fluctuations in population density. The linkage of markets in land, at best, is indirect, and hence land would only partially qualify as a true market commodity according to Polanyi's criterion.

The traditional method of selling land furnishes evidence of its non-participation in a market. In the original allocations, the zamindar forced the ryot to take barren land along with fertile land; the same practice continues today. In contrast, under a market system land is priced according to its value. Differing values will be reflected in differing prices. The assumption in a market economy is that at some price every commodity will find a buyer. But in a householding economy land unsuited to cultivation has no value in itself; hence it must be disposed of by tying it in with the sale of fertile land.

In summary, both a market economy and peasant economy employ price, but that is as far as the similarity extends, for the underlying mechanisms which govern prices in the two economies are entirely different. The price of land in a market economy responds to capitalized rent, while in a peasant economy, as Chayanov concluded, the price of land responds to the population density (Karblay, loc. cit.). This is the situation in Phulia Tola. As far back as its oldest inhabitants can remember, the price of village land has always risen, and this rise has been correlated with a steady rise in the population. Paradoxically, under conditions of high population density householding often raises the price of land above what it would be if it were being used as capital goods to produce a profit, for in the latter case the return on the produce might be so poor as actually to diminish its value (ibid.). The entrepreneur seeks a good return on his investment; to this end he considers the profit yield of various enterprises. For the peasant there are no alternatives : his goal is land for maintenance; for him land is not merely a commodity but a way of life.[1]

The same factor which explains the absence of a free market in land also explains the geographical and social unity of Phulia Tola. Land is of paramount importance in householding. The peasant clings tenaciously to land since it is the very basis of the

---

1. Since no product is intended for the market in a householding economy, terms used in a western economy, such as capital and profit, do not apply.

peasant economy, and the cultivation of land is the occupation for which he has been trained by a culture that is close to the soil. His security depends on his thorough knowledge of each of his plots — its drainage, its access to water, and its fertility. Many years of experience have taught him the best way to get the maximum yield from his acreage. This hard-won knowledge would be lost if he should move to another place. For this reason the peasant hangs onto his land. Since peasants must live close to their lands, both to cultivate them and to defend them, their habitations tend to cluster in the village at the center of their lands.

It will be recalled that the vast majority of the families in Phulia Tola were invited into the village by relatives for mutual aid and protection. The very arrangement of the houses, typical of so many Indian villages, reflects the kinship pattern. (Some people, of course, had to settle on the outskirts of the village when the original habitation site became crowded). Thus, today, as in the past, kinship is an important element of social cohesion in the village. In addition, the mere fact that a group of people live together in intimate contact with each other for generations, sharing the same problems and resolving them together, is sufficient to form strong social bonds.

Land and labor in relationship to a peasant economy have been discussed. Before examining the third component, capital, it is necessary to examine the role of the market in the economy of Phulia Tola. The town of Khagaul and its markets existed before the village was founded. In the early days, the sale of his poppy and milk provided the peasant with cash for the purchase of commodities and the payment of rent to the zamindar. To obtain enough money for rent was an accomplishment in itself, for the cost of living was then much lower — although the assessments were the same as today — and to meet the rent required a greater effort on the peasant's part. Later, when the price of milk started to rise, and land became more difficult to get, the market gave an opportunity for the poor man. He came to the village "to eat and to earn". At first he joined the household of a relative, until, by the sale of milk or services, he earned enough money to buy his own land and establish his own household. In doing this he followed community tradition : he set in motion a household economy. But the market had given him the means of establishing himself within such an economy. If you will, one of the terminals of a price-making market had been instrumental in spawning an economy of another kind. The model existed and the market provided the means to reproduce the peasant model. In this sense the presence of the market was partially responsible for the formation of the village.

The villagers' expression "to eat and to earn" expresses the symbiotic relationships that exist between the household and market economies. The villagers make it clear that the market provides a means of raising their standard of living above the level of a householding economy. Sri Krishun expressed this thought in the following way :

> In general, onions, potatoes, sugarcane is a special fund; money from potatoes, sugarcane is a special savings. Rice is eaten; if some rice is left over, the taxes are paid from it, like the land rent and the water tax. Milk pays for the daily expenses and clothing, and various expenditures come from the milk. But these onions, potatoes, sugarcane we can use for other things. This is the way of my village.*

In terms of the model, the products of the land are for maintenance. The "extras" provide for the standard of living beyond this. Sri Krishun includes potatoes and onions among cash crops but these have been brought into cultivation only recently. The improved standard of living of the village was made possible mainly through the sale of milk although poppy and sugarcane had some part in this too. As barren land was converted to fertile soil, new crops such as potatoes and onions were cultivated to provide a cash crop in place of milk. Crops were not the only substitute, however. Wage labor in the last thirty years has more and more come to be the means of obtaining needed cash.

Once the peasant has established a secure base in a householding economy, has satisfied his modest material wants, and added some small amenities to his daily existence, he seeks to

*Translated from Hindi, except the word 'special' which was said in English both times.

raise his standard of living further by enlarging his expenditures in areas involving social position and prestige. Such expenditures are most evident in marriage and wedding arrangements. Except for three families, and added increment of income was matched by a corresponding increment of consumption; none of it was saved. For most families, any land they bought became a part of their household base.

In Western society prestige derives from a high standard of living and the accumulation of wealth provides security; for the Indian peasant prestige is associated with the wedding complex, and security derives from a vested interest in land.

The Roy family's history and success have been previously detailed. The point to be emphasized here is one of contrast and one of similarity with the rest of the villagers. The Roys were socialized in the market; market terms and concepts are familiar to them and enter into their day-to-day activities. Their practice, for example, of renewing their herd of eight oxen every two years is motivated in part by a desire to enhance their prestige in the area and in part by a purpose which reveals their Western-oriented thinking : "to keep our capital intact."* Bihoren's adage, "money is like a stream which should be kept flowing," also shows a market orientation. This socialization differs markedly from the socialization of the average man raised in the village and gives the Roys an extra dimension, beyond that which Nash mentions as "increasing the scale of social relations [1966: 133]." Just as important as the extensiveness of their market relationships was the special nature of these relationships. It is the key to the unique position of the Roys in the village and their disdain of the village.

The social behavior of the Roys in contrast to that of the other villagers reflects the contrast of a petty bourgeois mentality and peasant mentalities. Most notable is the Roy's behavior with regard to marriage arrangements. They allocate for this purpose the profits of the dairy for a year. This excludes what they earn from their fields. On the other hand, a village family will spend as much money as it can obtain. Since marriage is the largest single item during the year which involves a cash outlay by the family, the Roys have in effect placed a limit on theirs, while the other families spend "up to their capacity."**

---

*Said in English.

**Translated from Hindi.

Consequently, in this regard the Roys systematically effect savings, and the village, for the most part, has none. The last two marriages of Roy girls illustrate the family's position on marriage expenditures. The first marriage, chronologically, was to a good looking, well educated boy from a well-to-do family from Patna. The Roys agreed to pay about 50 per cent more than their usual amount, but at the time of the wedding attempted to retreat to their customary figure. They were unsuccessful and had to pay, finally, the sum agreed upon. The next bridegroom was a boy of average looks and good education from a well-to-do family who lived on the Nepal border, about one hundred miles distant. The dowry was the Roys' customary amount. Presumably, the reason the Roys employed a professional *agua* (marriage broker) a Brahman, this time was in order to find an acceptable boy at their customary figure. As with all the items which collectively compose their standard of living, the amount of their dowries, while exceeding that of the other villagers by far, was much below what another family of their same wealth would have spent. Thus, their reluctance to maintain a standard of living commensurate with their wealth allows the Roys to accumulate money. Their petty bourgeois mentality is a function of their socialization in the market, just as the peasant's reflects his household upbringing in the balancing of production with consumption.

And yet the Roy family, at least the older generation, share with the village a most important value : their reliance on land. The dairy's function is to act like a machine which manufactures land for them. To them land is the ultimate security; and this desire for security in terms of land ultimately led them physically into the village and resulted in their becoming embedded, though reluctantly, in its culture.

In general, a peasant economy does not generate capital and does not provide a market for capital. The inherent character of householding, to consume what is produced, prevents saving and hence is inimical to a capital market, for the first step in the creation of capital is to withhold from consumption a certain amount of one's earnings. With a few possible exceptions, the villagers do not take this first step. In fact the contrary is true : the peasant economy is a drain on the capital market. When the peasant takes money earned in the market and buys land and so becomes a householder or extends his householding to keep up with the increasing size of his family, the money has gone from one type of economy and disappeared into another. Or if, as is usually the case, the peasant takes any "profit," he makes and uses it all to improve his standard of living, and the market economy suffers "leakage"—the opposite of capital investment. Furthermore, the peasant does not put any temporary accumulation of money into a bank; thus he denies the market the opportunity of channeling money to those who would use it for capital investment. The Roys do have a bank account, but the balance is kept low.

However, an argument could be made that land put into the production of crops is a capital improvement and hence that the peasant in Phulia Tola has created capital. The writer would deny this interpretation, for almost all the entire yield has gone into householding. The new families that have predictable crop surpluses and sell them could be considered part of the capital market. On the other hand, if there is any validity to Frank A. Fetter's definition of capital as "a conception of individual riches having real meaning only within the price system and in the market place where it originated, and developing with the spread of the financial calculus in business practice [1930:190, Vol. 3]," then none of the purchases of land could be regarded as eventuating in capital since none of the parties use any "financial calculus." This last statement applies to the Roy family, for while their standard of living is much higher than that of the other villagers, it falls far below the level of their social equals in town. Living in many respects close to the level of their neighbors they are able to accumulate money to purchase land and achieve the security which is the aim of every peasant. Parmeshwer Roy's remark that he would buy land today even if he knew the price would go down tomorrow shows this clearly. The Roys' attitude towards land reflects their peasant background.

The Roys had a choice; they could have taken all their profits and reinvested them in the dairy or some other business. The Dinapore branch of their family did go in the other direction, but only after they had accumulated much land. Both families have a foot in each economy. From the writer's limited acquaintance, this is a usual thing in India; the educated people he met usually belonged to well-to-do families all of whom had land in some village with a relative taking care of it, and, in addition, were to some degree part of a joint family.

The functioning of a peasant economy in a symbiotic relationship with a market as exemplified by Phulia Tola in its relations with Khagaul and Calcutta has perpetuated an eonomic system which has effectively resisted the accumulation of money for capital investment and the rise of capital markets. The point has been well made recently by Walter C. Neale :

> The reason why there were not satisfactory alternative uses for factors in the industrial and commercial spheres is a question beyond the compass of a history of the market for land. ... The essential point is clear : that India did not produce any appreciable number of entrepreneurs, did not produce a group of industrial capitalists or any substitute for them. Whatever the reason, there was *no alternative to the land.* When rents rise to the value of the marginal productivity of land, the next step would be an increase in the quantity of land and of substitutes for land, but in the absence of money and industrial capital markets there was no mechanism to make this secondary reaction to the rise of rents effective [1962:184]. [My emphasis — L.S.]

Neale's observations make it clear that the experience of the Roys and the villagers of Phulia Tola simply provide another example of the traditional economic and social patterns that persist in India today. The behavior of the inhabitants described in this paper supply the necessary details to support this view. The persistence of this pattern of socio-economic behavior at all levels of Indian society accounts, as Neale points out, for the failure of India itself to create industrial wealth. Conspicuous consumption at upper caste levels imitated by the lower castes in lavish display at weddings and other ceremonies uses up money which might have been accumulated for capital investment. The Roys furnish a typical example of the well-to-do Indian who departs from conventional ways of social and economic behavior. For it is obvious from the history of this family that they had opportunities to become true entrepreneurs in a market economy but that, governed by their peasant ambitions, they preferred to follow traditional paths which led them back at every step toward the land and directed all their actions to its accumulation and improvement.

The Roys exhibit the same peasant ambitions as the villagers and follow the same patterns of social and economic behavior. The differences between the Roys and the villagers are quantitative rather than qualitative. The Roys will spend more for a wedding, for education, and for the raising of their standard of living in other respects but not to a degree that brings their way of life into marked contrast with that of the village as a whole. Their economic interests are centered in the village but they are also townsmen in a sense, for it is in the town that they have their dairy and where they like to socialize and enjoy the prestige which the villagers attach to an Indian businessman. But the business remains a mere adjunct of their land interests. Their outlook remains that of the landholder.

The villager too remains land oriented. Where the choice between agricultural labor and industrial labor is offered, he will choose to work on the land. Ghosal has noted the persistence of this tendency in Indian history (1946:101). Any other work is regarded simply as a means of filling the needs which a household economy cannot always satisfy, or of providing cash income for the family when one of its members can be spared from work in the fields. In the same economic category as industrial labor are crops such as poppy, sugar cane, potatoes, and onions that are raised for the market in sufficient quantities to supply the peasant household with enough cash for incidental expenses. Thus the bahavior of the villagers of Phulia Tola is analogous to that of the Roys. In both cases, the economic activities are directed to the possession, ownership, and cultivation of land. The social patterns in which these activities are embedded persist along traditional lines.

The people of the village have had two prime avenues of communication and change. The first is that of kinship and caste affiliation, the second is that of the market. The market has provided the means for poor people to become more secure and for all to raise their standard of living. The writer predicts that the symbiotic relations between the market and the village will remain as long as the two economies operate side by side. The various household units will expand and contract; the personnel of the village will change, not only through births and deaths, but also by arrivals and departures, mostly the latter. At some point the maximum productive capacity of agriculture will be reached, and at that point few new people will settle in the village and natural increase will force some who are already settled to leave. Until the present, however, only two people are known to have left the village permanently, and they left a long time ago.

The writer's predictions as to what the future will bring are in part based on two assumptions : (1) once people become accustomed to a certain level of living, retreat to a lower level becomes difficult, and (2) emulation motivates people to climb higher in the social scale. Now that the richer families in Phulia Tola have electricity, no doubt others will want it too. In order to maintain or increase a standard of living which is visible in the market and in the village, additional efforts to increase production have to be made. The increase could be in the form of more cash crops, but such a change would undermine the very base of the economy and is therefore unlikely to go in that direction to any appreciable degree. For the economy would no longer be householding once it became dependent on cash crops and the market mechanism. In such a case, the likelihood is that the political structure of the household would remain, for the production and consumption unit would remain the same.

Actually the push has been to outside services and wage labor. The richer families have encouraged their children to get educated in order to get good jobs with the government. Naturally the Roy family is the foremost example of this. One of the extended family members told the writer :

> The man who is not educated, who hasn't anything, he farms, but he has education so he went for service.*

Probably education was always highly valued, but now with more families having the means to educate their children, education has become a mark of prestige.

While most joint families have adapted wage labor to householding, among some families wage labor has been the beginning of the dissolution of the household as an economically viable unit.

---

*Translated from Hindi.

When the source of a man's income is separate from his family's, the tendency is for that person to think of his earnings as belonging to himself and to his nuclear family rather than to the joint family. If he withholds money from the family purse, frictions develop. When a man must live away from home in order to work, this friction is aggravated, for he identifies himself less with the joint family and more with his nuclear family. Outside work promotes outside interests, social and economic. These frictions often result in the dissolution of the joint family. For the joint families which were poor to begin with, the separation into nuclear families destroys them as economically viable units. These are the families which are most likely to sell land and to become totally dependent eventually on wages. As Bailey has shown, "anyone who is forced to sell land to meet the cost of any ... contingency is on a descending spiral [1960:135]."

A small proportion of the families in the village are in such a condition. The Roy family in Nilkanth Tola was such a family — one that could barely maintain itself in the village. Such families are no longer householding; they have become true components of a market economy. They remain in the village because their home is there and the homesite is tax-free.

Whether the joint family is of poor or moderate means, the same frictions are likely to develop when a man lives away; but in the case of the family of moderate means, the sequence of events leading to separation will differ somewhat. It becomes difficult for a man living away from his family to hold on to his land unless he has somebody to work it and guard his crops from theft. The best solution for him will be to let it out to a tenant (tenancy being an intermediate step upward or downward), even with the knowledge that the tenant himself will steal from him. Eventually the need of money for a wedding or a funeral will force him first to mortgage his land and then to sell it. (Mortgaging is an intermediate step in buying or selling land). The buyer will be someone who lives in the village or has a relative in the village who will take care of the land. If his own natal family is the buyer, the household unit will remain the same. If the buyer is another family, it will gain at the seller's expense.

Obviously a family rich in land might buy the land, but it might also be a family which has little land but has a good income from wage labor in a place of employment close to the village. In such a case the market giveth and taketh away.

Of course the village has changed — economically and socially; however, the traditional economic pattern still predominates. Up to the present the new element, the market, has been absorbed and worked into the older economic mold. As long as the Indian peasant's economic base is land, the traditional economic pattern is likely to persist. This new element, insofar as Phulia Tola is concerned, is only new in the degree of involvement in the market. The increasing degree of participation in the market has resulted in prosperity for the village. In turn, while the prosperity has been manifest in a higher material standard of living, its thrust has been towards the elaboration of established socio-religious rites and customs. Both the elaboration and the selection of embellished traits was imitative of the upper castes.

The writer concludes that a peasant economy is hostile to a true market economy in land, labor, and capital. The same factors which are responsible for this antagonism also act to maintain the village as a social and geographical entity. Despite this, the town was instrumental in the founding and growth of the village. Participation in the market proved beneficial to a peasant economy and may, in fact, be considered a significant means of instituting it.

The market has had varying degrees of importance in the various stages of the village's development. In the latter stages it has been the means of support for new arrivals. The scrutiny of the market by this study, however, should not draw attention away from the primary source of support for the vast majority of arrivals at Phulia Tola — the family, whether consanguineal, affinal, or extended. This study reveals that kinship ties, and in particular gyno affiliations, more than any other factor were responsible for the replication of a typical Indian village in a virgin area. Kinship affiliation was the method of establishing the village of Phulia Tola and that within the kinship rubric, in a situation of patrilineality and village exogamy, gyno-locality was the important pattern which guided the members of the village.[1]

1. Murdock has elucidated the different kinds of data which become available when a processual, rather than a static, approach is used (1955:361-70).

It is not amiss to remember in these days when the "backward" nations wish to develop industrially that at one time man's ambition was to become a peasant:

> The Caste System seems to have worked in its inexorable way to create a fixed labour reserve force for agricultural production. Members of the low castes ... could never aspire to the status of peasants, holding or cultivating the land on their own. It would not ... be surprising if the actual status of many of them was semi-servile, involving a kind of bondage to a particular community of caste peasants or *zamindars* [Habib, 1963:122].

The Gowāllās in some places were a caste who had to do forced labor (Anon., 1924:7; Tallents, 1923:237); at least one man came to Phulia Tola to escape this, indicating the Gowāllās may have been one of the depressed castes. In general, the lower castes imitate the ways of the upper castes, and in particular we have followed up-casting among the Gowāllās; thus, it seems plausible that the Gowāllās were one of the lower castes who aspired to land and the way of life of the upper castes and seized any opportunity to realize these aspirations.

The writer has attempted to delineate the economic development of a north Indian village in its various aspects and ramifications. Many interesting problems, however, remain for future investigation : (1) the viability of a householding economy in an industrializing society; (2) the existence of villages that have followed a pattern of economic development similar to that of Phulia Tola; (3) the ratio of one-caste to multi-caste villages and the rationale of village caste patterns; (4) a comparison of the behavioral patterns in a one-caste village as opposed to a multi-caste pattern; (5) the function of national caste organizations as far as villages are concerned.

On the basis of the writer's observations, no significant change in the pattern of life is forseeable in the near future for Phulia Tola. Householding economy seems likely to continue in its traditional form along with the peripheral market relationship that helps to sustain it.

BIBLIOGRAPHY

Anonymous, 1912, Bihar and Orissa Police, Abstract of Intelligence. Volume I, No. 1, # 274.

Anonymous, 1912, Bihar and Orissa Police, Abstract of Intelligence. Volume I, No. 1, # 298.

Anonymous, 1912, Bihar and Orissa Police, Abstract of Intelligence. Volume I, No. 1, # 476.

Anonymous, 1915, Report on the Administration of Bihar and Orissa, 1913-1915. Patna, The Bihar and Orissa Secretariat Book Depot.

Anonymous, 1916, Report on the Administration of Bihar and Orissa, 1914-1915. Patna, The Bihar and Orissa Secretariat Book Depot.

Anonymous, 1923a, Report on the Trade Carried by Rail and River in Bihar and Orissa, 1921-22. Patna, Government Printing, Bihar and Orissa.

Anonymous, 1923b, Bihar and Orissa : First Decennial Review (1912-22). Patna, Government Printing, Bihar and Orissa.

Anonymous, 1924, Bihar and Orissa in 1923. Patna, Government Printing, Bihar and Orissa.

Anonymous, 1926, Bihar and Orissa in 1924-25. Patna, Government Printing, Bihar and Orissa.

Arensberg, Conrad M., 1962, Personal Communication.

———, 1957, Anthropology as History *In* Polanyi, Karl, Conrad M. Arensberg and Harry W. Pearson (eds.), Trade and Market in the Early Empires, Glencoe, Free Press, 97-113.

———, 1966, Cultural Change and Guaranteed Income *In* Theobald, Robert (ed.), Garden City, Doubleday, 199-233.

Aschmann, Homer, 1965, Comments on the Symposium *In* Leeds, Anthony and Andrew P. Vayda (eds.), Man, Culture, and Animals. Washington, D.C., American Advancement of Science, 259-270.

Ayres, C. E., 1966, Guaranteed Income : An Institutional View *In* Theobald, Robert (ed.), The Guaranteed Income. Garden City, Doubleday, 162-174.

Bailey, F. G., 1958, Caste and the Economic Frontier. Manchester University Press.

———, 1960, An Oriya Hill Village II *In* Srinivas, M. N. (ed.) India's Villages. New York, Asia Publishing House, Second edition. Publishing House (second edition), 131-146.

Baines, J. A., 1893, General Report, Census of India, 1891. London, Eyre and Spottiswoode.

Barth, Frederik, 1966, Models of Social Organization (Occasional paper No. 23). London, Royal Anthropological Institute of Great Britain and Ireland.

Beidelman, Thomas O., 1959, A Comparative Analysis of the Jajmani System. Locust Valley, J. J. Augustin.

Belshaw, C. B., 1965, Traditional Exchange and Modern Markets. Englewood Cliffs, Prentice Hall.

Boeke, J. H., 1953, Economics and Economic Policy of Dual Societies. New York, Institute of Pacific Relations.

Bourdillon, J. A., 1883, Report on the Census of Bengal, 1881. Calcutta, Bengal Secretariat Press.

Buyers, William, 1848, Recollections of Northern India, London, John Snow.

Choudhary, Radhakrishna, 1958, History of Bihar. Patna, Motilal Banarsidass.

The College Standard Dictionary, 1940. New York, Funk and Wagnalls.

Davidson, Edward, 1868, The Railways of India. London, E. and F. B. Spon.

Davis, Kingsley, 1951, The Population of India and Pakistan. Princeton, Princeton University Press.

Dutt, Shoshee C., 1884, Bengal. London, Gilbert and Rivington.

Dalton, George (ed.), 1968, Primitive, Archaic and Modern Economies. Garden City, Doubleday Anchor.

Epstein, T. S., 1962, Economic Development and Social Change in South India. Manchester, University Press.

Fetter, Frank A., 1930, Capital *In* Seligman, Edwin R. A. (ed.), Encyclopedia of the Social Sciences Volume 3, New York, Macmillan 187-190.

Firminger, Walter K. (ed.), 1917, The Fifth Report. Vol. II. Introduction and Bengal Appendiced. Calcutta, R. Cambray Reprinted.

Firth, Raymond, 1951, Elements of Social Organization. London, Watts.

Firth, Raymond and B. S. Yamey (eds.), 1964, Capital, Savings and Credit in Peasant Societies. London, Allen and Unwin.

Foster, George M., 1967, Introduction : What is a Peasant ? *In* Potter, Jack M., May n. Diaz, and George M. Foster. Peasant Society. Boston, Little, Brown 2-13.

Gatt, E. A., 1902, Census of India, 1901, Volume VI — Bengal, Part I, Report. Calcutta, Bengal Secretariat Press, 1902.

———, 1913, Census of India, 1911, Part I, Report. Calcutta, Government Printing.

Ghosal, Hari R., 1946, Price Change and Price Control in India During the Last Two Hundred Years. The Journal of the Bihar Research Society. Patna, 32:297-307.

Ghosal, Hari R., 1946, Labour in Early Nineteenth Century, Bihar. The Journal of the Bihar Research Society. Patna, 32:98-105.

Habib, Irfan, 1963, The Agrarian System of Mughal India (1556-1707). New York, The Asia Publishing House.

Harper, Edward B., 1959, Two Systems of Economic Exchange in Village India. American Anthropologist 61:760-778.

Harris, Marvin, 1959, The Economy has no Surplus ? American Anthropologist; 61:185-199.

———, 1965, The Myth of the Sacred Cow *In* Leeds, Anthony And Andrew P. Vayda (eds.), Man, Culture, and Animals. Washington, D.C., The Advancement of Science.

———, 1966, The Cultural Ecology of India's Sacred Cattle. Current Anthropology, 7:51-65.

Heilbroner, Robert L., 1967, The Wordly Philosophers, third edition. New York, Simon and Schuster.

Hoselitz, Bert F., 1961, Tradition and Economic Growth *In* Braibanti, Ralph and Joseph J. Spengler (eds.), Tradition, Values, and Socio-economic Development. Durham, Duke University Press, 85-113.

Hunter, W. W., 1886, London, Trubner, second edition.

Hutton, J. H., 1933, Census of India, 1931. Volume I — India, Part I. Report. Delhi, Manager of Publications.

———, 1961, Caste in India. London, Oxford University Press, third edition.

Houlton, Sir John, 1949, Bihar the Heart of India. New York, Longmans, Green.

Jackson, J. W. C., 1929, Bihar and Orissa in 1927-28. Patna, Government Printing, Bihar and Orissa.

James, John Francis William, 1914, Final Report on the Survey and Settlement Operations in the District of Patna, 1907-1912. Patna, Bihar and Orissa Government Press.

Kale, Vaman G., Introduction to the Study of Indian Economics. Poona : Aryabhushan Press, 1920 (3d ed.).

———, 1920, Introduction to the Study of Indian Economics. Poona : Aryabhushan Press, third edition.

Karve, Irawati, 1961, Hindu Society. Poona, Deccan College.

Karblay, Basile, 1966, A. V. Chayanov : Life, Career, Works *In* Thorner, Daniel, Basile Karblay and R. E. F. Smith (eds.), A. V. Chayanov on the Theory of Peasant Economy. Homewood, The American Economic Association, xxv-lxxv.

Khedkar, Vithal K., 1959, The Divine Heritage of the Yadavas. Allahabad, Parmanand.

Klass, Morton, 1961, East Indians in Trinidad. New York, Columbia University Press.

———, 1966, Marriage Rules in Bengal. American Anthropologist, 68:951-970.

Lacey, W. G., 1928, Bihar and Orissa in 1926-27. Patna, Government Printing, Bihar and Orissa.

———, 1933, Census of India, 1931. Volume 7, Bihar and Orissa, Part I, Report. Patna, Government Printing.

Leeds, Anthony, 1961, The Port-of-Trade in Pre-European India as an Ecological and Evolutionary Type *In* Garfield, Viola E. (ed.), Symposium : Patterns of Land Utilization. Seattle, American Ethnological Society, 26-48.

Levi-Strauss, Claude, 1953, Social Structure *In* Kroeber, A. L. (ed.), Anthropology today. Chicago, University of Chicago Press, 524-553.

Lynch, Owen M., 1968, The Politics of Untouchability — the Case from Agra, India *In* Singer, Milton and Bernard S. Cohn (eds.), Structure and Change in Indian Society. New York, Viking Fund Publications in Anthropology No. forty-seven, 209-240.

Malinowski, Bronislaw, 1922, Argonauts of the Western Pacific. London, George Routledge.

Mandelbaum, David G., 1968, Family, *Jāti*, Village *In* Singer, Milton and Bernard S. Cohn (eds.), Structure and Change in Indian Society. New York, Viking Fund Publications in Anthropology number forty-seven, 29-50.

Manners, Robert A., 1965, The Kepsigis — Change with Alacrity *In* Bohannan, Paul and George Dalton (eds.), Markets In Africa. Garden City, The Natural History Library, 214-249.

Martin, J. T., 1921, Census Report, 1921. Calcutta, Government Printing.

Martin, Montgomery, 1838, The History, Antiquities, Topography, and Statistics of Eastern India. Volume I. London, William H. Allen.

Moore, Wilbert E., 1961, The Social Framework of Economic Development *In* Braibanti, Ralph, and Joseph J. Spengler (eds.), Traditions, Values, and Socio-Economic Development, 57-82.

———, 1965, The Impact of Industry. Englewood Cliffs, Prentice Hall.

Moreland, W. H., 1912, The Agriculture of the United Provinces. Allahabad, Government Press.

———, 1914, Notes on the Agricultural Conditions and Problems of the United Provinces. Allahabad, Government Press.

——— ,1917, Prices and Wages Under Akbar, Journal of the Royal Asiatic Society of Great Britain and Island, 815-825.

Moreland, W. H. and Atul C. Chatterjee, 1945, A Short History of India. London, Longmans, Green.

Murray, C. R. B., 1930, Bihar and Orissa in 1928-29. Patna, Government Printing, Bihar and Orissa.

Mukerjee, Radhakamal, 1916, The Foundations of Indian Economies. New York, Longmans, Green.

———, 194 ?, The Economic History of India : 1600-1800. New York, Longmans, Green.

Murdock, George F., 1955, Changing Emphases on Social Science, Southwestern Journal of Anthropology, 11:361-70.

Nair, Kusum, 1961, Blossoms in the Dust. London, Gerald Duckworth.

Narain, Bris, 1929, Indian Economic Life. Lahore, Uttar Chand Kapur.

Nanavati, Manilal B. and J. J. Anjaria, 1957, Indian Rural Problems. Bombay, Vura, fourth edition.

Nash, Manning, 1966, Primitive and Peasant Economic Systems, San Francisco, Chandler.

Neale, Walter C., 1957, Reciprocity and Redistribution in the Indian Village *In* Polanyi, Karl, Conrad M. Arensberg, and Harry Pearson (eds.), Trade and Markets in the Early Empires. Glencoe, Free Press, 218-236.

———, 1962, Economic Change in Rural India. New Haven, Yale University Press.

O'Malley, L. S. S., 1907, Bengal District Gazetteers, Patna,. Calcutta, The Bengal Secretariat Book Depot.

———, 1932, Indian Caste Customs. Cambridge, University Press.

———, 1941, The Hindu Social System *In* O'Malley, L. S. S. (ed.), Modern India and the West. London, Oxford University Press.

Owen, G. E., 1922, Bihar and Orissa in 1921. Patna, Government Printing, Bihar and Orissa.

Polanyi, Karl, 1957a, The Great Transformation. Boston, Beacon Press.

———, 1957b, The Economy as Instituted Process *In* Polanyi, Karl, Conrad M. Arensberg, and Harry Pearson (eds.), Trade and Markets in the Early Empires. Glencoe, The Free Press, 243-269.

———, 1966, Dahomey and the Slave Trade. Seattle, American Ethnological Society Monograph 42.

Radhakamal, Mukerjee, n.d. [194 ?], The Economic History of India : 1600-1800. New York, Longmans, Green.

Ramsbotham, R. B., 1926, Studies in the Land Revenue History of Bengal 1769-1787. London, Humphrey Milford, Oxford University Press.

Raye, N. N., 1927, The Annals of the Early English Settlement in Bihar. Calcutta, Sachindralal Mitra.

Redfield, Robert, 1956, Peasant Society and Culture. Chicago, University of Chicago Press.

Rosenfield, Henry, 1958, Process of Structural Change Within the Arab Village Extended Family. American Anthropologist 60:1127-1139.

Sankar, Jadunath, 1913, Economics of British India. Calcutta, M. C. Barker, third edition.

Srinivas, M. N., 1962, Caste in Modern India. Calcutta, Asia Publishing House.

——— (ed.), 1963, India's Villages. Calcutta, Asia Publishing House.

Swartzberg, Leon Jr., 1967, The Instrumentalities and results of Entrepreneurship in a North Indian Family. M. A. Thesis, Columbia University, New York.

Tallents, P. C., 1923, Census of India, 1921. Volume VII Bihar and Orissa, Part I, Report. Patna, Government Printing, Bihar and Orissa.

Thorner, Daniel, 1966, Chayanov's Concept of Peasant Economy *In* Thorner, Daniel, Basile Karblay and R. E. F. Smith (eds.), A. V. Chayanov on the Theory of Peasant Economy. Homewood, The American Economic Association, xi-xxiii.

Thorner, Daniel and Alice, 1962, Land and Labour in India. Calcutta, Asia Publishing House.

Thorton, Edward, 1957, A Gazetteer of the Territories Under the Government of the East-India Company. London, William H. Allen.

Veblen, Thorsten, 1931, The Theory of the Leisure Class. New York, Modern Library, reprinted.

Von Dietz, C., 1937, Peasantry *In* Seligman, Edwin R. A. (ed.), Encyclopaedia of the Social Sciences, Volume 12. New York, Macmillan re-issued, 48-53.

Whitehead, Alfred North, 1958, Adventure of Ideas. New York, New American Library.

Wolf, Eric R., 1966, Peasants. Englewood-Cliffs, Prentice Hall.

INDEX

CORRECTIONS

Page	*Line*	*For*	*Read*
27	2	well-	well
30	fn. 1	Swartsberg	Swartzberg
32	20	non	none
33	7 from below	prohibited	were prohibited
43	1	Pradad Bhagat,	Prasad Bhagat and
45	9 from below	no clear	not clear
46	21	there;	there,
55	17	elaiming	claiming
56	4	most sensitive	more sensitive
71	9	lobor	labor
111	22	[12]	[1]
114	10	distain	disdain
123	11 from below	peasnt	peasant
126	3	noteworth	noteworthy
151	5	eonomic	economic